I Love You

I LOVE YOU

But God Loves You More

Nina Pringle

MICAH 6:8
BOOKS

Published in Pinole, California by:
Micah 6:8 Books, LLC
P.O. Box 12
Pinole, CA 94564

Scripture quotations are taken from the Holy Bible, King James Version®.

This is a work of nonfiction. The views and recommendations are drawn from the author's life experiences and beliefs.

ISBN: 0-9897968-9-2
ISBN13: 978-0-9897968-9-7

Cover Design: Tywebbin Creations
Cover Photo: Cecil A. Phillips, Jr.

First Printing, 2020

Printed in the United States of America

Dedication

Rachel Pringle-Logan, Demetrius Pringle, Sr.,
Casey Pringle, Jr.,

New Testament Holy Church of Jesus Youth

&

Your Peers

I love you with all of my heart!

Contents

Acknowledgements

To my dear husband and Pastor, Casey L. Pringle, Sr., without you I would have never found true love and happiness. I am eternally grateful to you and will never find another man as compassionate as you. You are just as much a part of this book as I am because I would have never found the truth nor come to love God as much as I do without your teaching and exemplary life. I love you beyond measure. I will forever be grateful to you for the knowledge and inspiration that you have imparted to me.

I would like to give a special thank you and acknowledgement to the late, Bishop Casey Pringle, for leaving such a wonderful, life-saving legacy. I shall forever love you and be grateful to you for your wisdom and profound knowledge of God's word. From your favorite scripture in Psalms, you would always say, "This is the man that I long to be." Judging from the respect and the love that surrounded you, I would say that you came closer than anyone that I have ever known to being that man.

"BLESSED is the man that walketh not in the counsel of the ungodly, nor standeth in the way of sinners, nor sitteth in the

seat of the scornful. But his delight is in the law of the Lord; and in his law doth he meditate day and night. And he shall be like a tree planted by the rivers of water, that bringeth forth his fruit in his season; his leaf also shall not wither; and whatsoever he doeth shall prosper. The ungodly are not so: but are like the chaff which the wind driveth away. Therefore the ungodly shall not stand in the judgment, nor sinners in the congregation of the righteous. For the Lord knoweth the way of the righteous: but the way of the ungodly shall perish."
Psalm 1

I love you, my children and New Testament youth! Your father/Pastor and I have set a very good example of how you all ought to live both in the natural and the spirit. I pray that one day before it's too late you will prove this to be true and receive Jesus Christ into your heart and soul!

As I have tried to understand your behaviors and attitudes and that of your peers, I have said, and many others say, "That it is the generation that we live in now." Although that is true, I also believe that it is because you all haven't allowed Jesus Christ to come fully into your lives. I know that times are different and the world has changed: people have gotten wiser and technology has taken over. But Jesus Christ is the same according to Hebrews 13:8, *Jesus Christ the same yesterday, and today, and for ever.* We don't have to be like the people of the world we can live better lives and be better people. We can be joyful and happy in spite of all the negativity and destruction going on in the world around us. I see all that you all are subjected to. You have everything that your heart can desire at your fingertips and it's not good it's the trick of the enemy to keep you bound and confused. I love you all, beloved ones, but I have to tell you, you need to seek the Lord as never before.

As you have inspired me to write this book, I hope

that this book will inspire you to seriously consider developing a personal relation with Jesus Christ. Please enjoy reading this book and know that it comes from a place of love for you and your peers.

"Remember now thy creator in the days of thy youth, while the evil days come not, nor the years draw nigh, when thou shalt say, I have no pleasure in them. While the sun, or the light, or the moon, or the stars, be not darkened, nor the clouds return after the rain." **Ecclesiastes 12:1-2**

Introduction

Beloved, let me start by saying that I love you. I truly do, and I want you to be happy now in this life and for eternity. I am concerned for your soul. I am sorry that I cannot give you a motivational speech such as you may be used to hearing. Time is too far spent for me to waste it telling you about all of the good stuff that this world has to offer you. My purpose in reaching out to you is to let you know the truth as to why you have life and how you are supposed to live it.

Jesus wants you to know how to save your soul from hell. Young people are dying every day. The news is filled with violence. Prison cells are full. Men are marrying men and likewise women. So many young people are lost to this dying world. Things are not going to get any better. Your only hope is in turning your life over to Jesus.

I want you to really learn what the will of the Lord is for your life. I want you to really hear what I am saying: **God loves you!** He gave his Son's life for you. You in turn have to love him – Jesus, who is now your intercessor with God. This is not difficult beloved ones. Read your Bible, pray, establish a relationship with Jesus. Then find a good Bible based church and commit to serving the Lord.

I take this ministry seriously and would be amiss if I did not do all that I could to help save souls for the Kingdom of God. Your life is precious and you should live it to the greatest of your ability unto the Lord. Your soul can not die, it will live for eternity either in heaven or in hell. It is your choice to decide where you will live eternally, but you have to decide now before it is too late. I hope to persuade you to choose heaven. If I fail, and you ignore my plea, you are destine for hell where there is pain, suffering, misery, and continual hell fire. Will you ponder this question in your mind and heart for a minute: How shall I escape hell? The answer is: through Jesus Christ our Lord and Savior.

I want you to understand that whether or not you believe, accept, or obey God's word, it will come to pass. I pray that as you read you will have an open mind and heart to receive this beautiful message from God – it will save your life. Open your heart and mind to God and take full advantage of your life. I love you all so much that I am willing to come out of my comfort zone and speak to you from the core of my soul in hopes that someone – if only one – will change his or her life and come to Christ.

Again, I would be amiss if I did not tell you the truth and it would be a waste of my time and yours. God loves you. He has made great sacrifices for you and all that He asks in return is that you love Him. So, I plead with you, seek the Lord now with all of your heart while you still have time. If you don't read anything else beyond this introduction, please, please learn how to love the Lord with all of your heart, mind, body, soul, and strength. I cannot let your blood be required at my hand nor do I want to see you suffer any longer in this life when I know there is a better way for you to live here and in eternity.

So thou, O son of man, I have set thee a watchman unto the house of Israel; therefore thou shalt hear the word at my mouth, and warn them from me. When I say unto the wicked, O wicked man, thou shalt surely die; if thou dost not speak to warn the wicked from his way, that wicked man shall die in his iniquity; but his blood will I require at thine hand. Nevertheless, if thou warn the wicked of his way to turn from it, if he do not turn from his way, he shall die in his iniquity; but thou hast delivered thy soul. Therefore, O thou son of man, speak unto the house of Israel; Thus ye speak, saying, if our transgressions and our sins be upon us, and we pine away in them, how should we then live? Say unto them, As I live, saith the Lord GOD, I have no pleasure in the death of the wicked; but that the wicked turn from his way and live: turn ye, turn ye from your evil ways; for why will ye die, O house of Israel?
Ezekiel 33:7-11

Chapter 1

I Love You

I may not know you, but I love you. I love you with the love of God. I know that my love does not compare to the love that God and His Son, Jesus Christ, has for you. God is love. Jesus is the personification of God, and I am His humble servant. God has allowed me to receive a portion of His great love and I want to share it with you. I know and understand the great love that God has for you, I can feel it in my soul and it compels me to speak to you from my heart. The most quoted and familiar scripture of the Bible states: *For God so loved the world, that He gave his only begotten son, that whosoever believeth in him should not perish, but have everlasting life* (John 3:16).

God loved us so much that He sent His son Jesus Christ to die for our sins that we may have eternal life in Him. I hope to express the love of God in a manner that you will desire it too. I believe that I have eternal life in Christ Jesus because I believe Jesus to be the Son of God. I believe to the point that I now live a purposeful life serving God. I believe in Jesus who was crucified on Calvary's cross and now sits on the right hand of God the Father. I believe, if you will give God a chance, you too will become a believer. I love Him with all my heart, nothing nor anyone comes before my love for Him. I know that He suffered and died for me, and I know He didn't have to. I have never seen Jesus, but I have gained faith through reading the Word of God that He is my Lord and Savior and that He will come again to receive His people back into His Kingdom.

I see the lives that young people live, and I want so badly for them to receive salvation and the joy of the Lord before it's too late. My heart is heavy and grieves for you, beloved ones. I can just imagine how God feels in His heart about the loss state of mankind because I know how I feel about my loved ones – the youth. From my observations, today's youth lack joy. I know they could live a happier life. The love and validation they appear to be seeking can't be found in the things, nor in the people they are chasing after. We all need an intimate relationship with God and His Son, Jesus Christ. The more we commune with God, the more we will discover we don't need to seek after people and things. What we are seeking will be right in front of us. God is our creator, and we have an inherent need for a relationship with Him. Until we develop that relationship with God, we will continue to look in all the wrong places for what we need. God has given explicit instructions on how to receive Him and eternal life; start by reading the Bible and praying to ask God for clarification of His Word and then find someone who can explain it further to you.

God's will for our life is that we love Him with all of our heart, mind, soul, and strength and that we obey His commandments. Until we – young and old – establish a relationship with Jesus, we will remain in a lost state of sin. This concept may sound foreign, or strange, but it is real. Heaven and hell are real and we will have to go to one or the other one day. Why not be prepared and make a conscience decision as to where you want to spend eternity. You may not believe or fully believe in God, heaven, hell, or the ever after, but are you willing to take a chance with your life? If there is a chance that you could live a better life here and now, wouldn't it be worth your consideration to try and find out how to do that? Through this book, I endeavor to help you prepare yourself for the Kingdom of God and to encourage you along the way. It excites me to be able to write this book, hopefully for all the world to read and learn of God's goodness.

We were not created to live on this earth and hell was not created for mankind. We were created to live in a Holy place: The Garden of Eden. *Therefore the Lord God sent him forth from the garden of Eden, to till the ground from whence he was taken . . . (*Genesis 3:23).

God created Adam to live in a world without pain, loss, and confusion. A place where love, joy, and peace create the perfect atmosphere. We – mankind – were created to live with God in Eden, not knowing any evil, until Adam disobeyed. Hell was originally prepared for Satan and the fallen angels. Since Adam and Eve's fall from grace, hell has enlarged. *Therefore hell hath enlarged herself, and opened her mouth without measure: and their glory, and their multitude, and their pomp, and he that rejoiceth, shall descend into it* . . . (Isaiah 5:14).

Those who die unsaved and out of the will of God are referred to as wicked, and will also spend eternity in hell. *The wicked shall be turned into hell, and all the nations that forget God* (Psalms 9:17). God could have, and rightfully so as our creator, left us in that fallen state or destroyed mankind all together but, God is love. God loves us so much that He sacrificed His only begotten Son that we may have eternal life, and enjoy abundant life on earth.

The Word of God gives comfort in the time of need. His word brings peace in the midst of turmoil. His word will save you from hell, if you believe it. His word is your road map to heaven. Most people don't believe hell exists but it does. And the only way to escape it is to accept Jesus Christ as Lord and Savior. Consider for a moment hell does exist and ask yourself, "Am I ready to leave this world unprepared?" If the answer is no, then please keep reading with an open mind and an earnest desire to know the truth.

By studying the Word of God, I have discovered the great things God has stored up for us in Heaven. Things that eyes have not seen, and ears have not heard. You have a great opportunity to learn of God's will at an early age so that you don't have to suffer this life without hope.

When I read Psalms 119:89, *Forever, O Lord, thy word is settled in heaven,* it confirmed in my soul that this was the true Word of God and that He would stand on His word. I knew that if I followed the Word of God that I would one day be with Him in Heaven.

I was raised in a large family of twelve children and two parents. We never saw a hungry day, we never lacked a roof over our heads, nor did we ever see a day that we didn't have shoes on our feet and clothes on our backs. We had good parents that raised us the old fashion way with a strong hand, morals, and love. However, as a teenager, I went through depression, rebellion, and in search of life as most teenagers do. Being an extremely quiet and shy person, I held everything in. I did have one close girlfriend to talk to, but I wasn't comfortable enough to tell her about the things that I wanted in life at that time. And I wasn't comfortable talking to my siblings, thinking that they would tell my parents. So, the stress of being a teenager took a toll on my body. When I turned seventeen, I started to suffer back and severe hip pain to the point that I couldn't walk the stage at my graduation. I had to finish high school at home with a tutor.

When my mother brought me home from the doctor, being a teenager, I misunderstood what the doctor had told my mother about my condition, and I decided then that I was not going to marry because I didn't want my husband to have to take care of me. I didn't want that kind of life for me or for my husband. It was bad enough that I had to suffer, I didn't want to make anyone else suffer with me. I thought that I would end up in a wheelchair one day. My lower back would ache so bad and I had pain that would go from one hip to the other. When I sat my foot down on the floor it felt as if I had a pinched nerve and the sharp pain would hit my hip and go down my leg. I walked as if I had one leg shorter than the other. It was almost impossible to walk up and down stairs, I had to take one stair at a time using my good leg at that time. Thank you, Jesus, that I am whole and healthy today.

When my mother found out that I was avoiding my boyfriend, who is now my husband, she talked to me and further explained my condition to me and convinced me to call him. I had been diagnosed by three different doctors with three different illnesses. The illness was exacerbated by the stress that I put on myself. I know that to be true because when I stress now, I can feel the pain returning. That's when I know that I have to turn whatever it is that I am stressing about over to the Lord. When I turn it over to the Lord and stop stressing about it, He works it out in my favor. I have learned that I can't do it all by myself. I have to lean on Jesus for my every need. He has never let me down and if you will lean on Him, He won't let you down either.

I didn't find true meaning to life and happiness until I got married and my husband introduced me to the Lord. He began to tell me to read the Bible and pray to the Lord for the healing of my pain. About seven months into our marriage after my husband convinced me that God would heal me if I believed in Him, I became pregnant. By then the pain was so minimal and sporadic, I didn't have to take any pain medication while pregnant. My trust in God enabled me to carry my son the full nine months. I didn't have to harm him with all of the pain medication that I had previously taken to minimize the pain. Praying to God, reading the Bible and with my husband's teaching, I was healed and became a true believer in God.

So, it wasn't a tragedy or a horrible life that brought me to the Lord. I received deliverance by way of seeking relief from the physical pain in my body. When I took heed to the word of God, repented for my sins, and accepted Christ Jesus as my Savior, I started to understand life and why I am here on earth. I know and believe with all of my heart that I was created to give God glory with my life. I am so thankful to have the knowledge and understanding that God is my creator and that I am to serve Him with all of my heart. I understand that this world is not my home. We are just passing through on our way back to our final and eternal destination. I understand that we are born, we live, and we die. It is just that simple. The difficult part seems to be knowing what to do with our time on Earth. The rest of my time will be spent trying to get others to believe in Jesus.

I decided the Word of God was true and right and wanted to live for the Lord because I heard the Word of God taught by my husband and Bishop and knew this was a life I wanted to live. I listened to the Word of God with an open mind and heart and it made so much good sense to me. I had experienced God working in my life through healing and found joy and peace of mind in the process. I made up my mind and I haven't turned back. There is no way that I can turn back into the world. Simply, because I love and trust God. I know that if I turn back, I would be lost forever. And furthermore, there is nothing in this world that I have a desire for more than to live a life in Christ Jesus knowing that I am securing my eternal future and providing peace for myself while I live.

As I studied the Bible and was taught with understanding, I discovered every aspect of life as I had lived it, or had questions about, was found in the Word of God. I have not found a straighter truth or reason for our being here in this painful, confused, destructive, dying world. So, while I live, I will serve the Lord to the best of my ability. If you read this book through, now you have no excuse to not live your life to the best of your ability.

God created mankind for His use, not ours. Following God's plan for mankind brings order and frees us from a hopeless and mundane life. The reason we are here on Earth as human beings is because God wanted to fill a void that was in the earth. *In the beginning, God created the heaven and the earth. And the earth was without form, and void . . . (*Genesis 1:1-2) *. . .male and female created he them . . . Be fruitful, and multiply, and replenish the earth, and subdue it: and have dominion . . .* (Genesis 1:26-28).

We were originally created holy and without sin designed to fill the earth for God's glory. All other things and creations were made for us (man) to reign over for God. As God is the creator and we are the creation we are to love and reverence Him. We are the creation that He is most proud of and He wants good things for us. Because God loves us so much, He sent His son, Jesus Christ, for us (man) to have a way back to Him, to heaven.

Most people have heard the story of Adam and Eve, and know that sin entered into the world by their disobedience, leaving the world in the horrible shape it is today. When the first man Adam fell from grace it caused every human being of his decent to be conceived in sin. From the fall of Adam up until now the hearts of men have become filled with evil. Many people have turned away from God. This world is in a place that is far worse than it was when God destroyed it the first time in Noah's day – Luke 17:26-27. I believe the Bible, and I believe God is grieved and so sickened with how Satan has captivated the minds of the people, that it won't be too much longer before God destroys this earth again.

You may not believe that God is going to destroy this world one day soon. Soon may not be in my lifetime or yours, but whenever He does, it will be too soon. The real issue for us is that we don't know what hour or day we will die and leave this earth, forever, so, beloved one, you need to get your soul right with the Lord now. So many young people are leaving this world without warning. Mothers are grieving for their children every day because their lives are being taken from them suddenly. Beloved ones, we don't know from one day to the next if we are going to live another day. The scripture even tells us tomorrow is not promised. We see this truth with our friends and family members. It doesn't have to happen to you – you don't have to be a victim of Satan's devices.

God has given us every opportunity to surrender our lives to Him and has laid a clear path for us to receive salvation. There will be no excuse when that time comes. I am so grateful and blessed to have found the truth, and if you will allow me, I will try and help you understand that this world is not your home and that there is a better place for you to spend eternity. I have found truth and it has given me a true love in my heart for you. Most precious of all, it has given me peace of mind in a world where there is no peace without the love of God. What I have found is immeasurable to anything in this world.

I have a wonderful husband of thirty-seven years. We are still in love and recently renewed our wedding vows. Neither of us has ever committed adultery. We have a wonderful relationship and have always put God first in our lives and at the center of our marriage. My husband taught me that nothing comes before God, not him or our children. Neither of our three children have ever been in jail, or addicted to drugs or alcohol. I thank God for that in this day and time, I know that it is a blessing. Young people now days seem to have lost all consciousness about the way they live their lives. Satan has deceived their minds by making them believe same-sex relationships are okay, pre-marital sex is expected, adultery is acceptable, and the use of drugs and alcohol is sociable. None of these lies are acceptable to God. He is not pleased with the way you are living your lives. You only have to give God a chance and see that He will fill your every need. He will give you the desires of your heart.

You may think that I am fabricating my life's story, but I am not. God has been so good to me! I know people that have turned their backs on God because of the loss of a loved one. There is no way that I can do that – God is the only reason that I have these loved ones in the first place. And I am so grateful that I have had them for as long as I have. If or when they are taken from me, I still have to give God the glory that is due His name and thank Him for the time that I had them in my life. Scripture says, *O taste and see that the LORD is good* (Psalms 34:8). Once you have tasted the goodness of the Lord, meaning received the spirit and the blessings of the Lord, I don't believe that one can turn away from that. I know that there are people that have said that they were once saved/sanctified and then turned back into the world due to various reasons, but I don't believe that those people crossed the separation line into Holiness.

I know too much about Him and His Word. There is a saying, "Once you learn better you do better." I have learned better and I strive every day to do better. I want my life to be pleasing to the Lord in everything that I do, so I try to make it a purpose every day to live it accordingly. I have lived my life so that I don't have any enemies, but if I did, I would pray for them and I would love them too. This life is so real and it takes a real God in your life to make it through each day without wanting to give up. I have found truth and God and I know that if I ask believing, I will receive. I put all of my confidence in the Lord because there is none else that can love me the way that He does. There is no one else that can do for me what He does, and there is no none else that can save me the way that He can.

Before you think that living a life that is pleasing to the Lord every day cannot be done, let me just say, "Yes it can!" *I can do all things through Christ which strengtheneth me* (Philippians 4:13). If God said for us to live holy then we can live holy. All you have to do is make up your mind to do it and seek the help of the Lord. He will send someone into your life that will teach you and encourage you to live the best life that you can live in Christ Jesus. I wouldn't tell you to do something that I don't feel is possible, but because I have done it and do it every day, I know that you too can do it! Believe that it is possible. Believe that you serve a God that has all power in his hands and that He made Heaven and Earth and all that is therein. It's all a matter of choice, beloved one, choose that which is good and good for you. You deserve to live in peace here and for eternity.

God made the stars, the moon, etc., He can cause you

to live holy and sanctified if you want to in this present world amongst all that is going on in the world. All that you have to do is put your faith and belief into action and know that God is Lord over your life! It really is that easy, believe and trust God to lead you to a better life in Christ Jesus. You may make a mistake but that does not mean that you are not living a holy life before the Lord. As long as you follow the Word of God and keep His commandments -which are not grievous – and love Him with all of your heart then you are living a holy, saved, sanctified life in Jesus. The Holy Ghost will lead and guide you to do the right things each day.

You have to believe and seek God for yourself. The majority of the human race will believe whatever they are taught, which is why so many people are lost and gone astray. You have to read and study. You cannot be influenced by God's word if you do not spend adequate time getting to know Him by reading His word. Over the past thirty-seven years, I have learned enough to save my life and reach out to others. I have asked God for revelation and understanding of His Word and He has given me some. I don't know what kind of life I would be living or what kind of person I would be if I didn't have God leading and guiding me, but I do know that it wouldn't be anywhere close to the wonderful life that I live today or the joy that I have in my soul.

I wish that I would have come to this point in my life at an even younger age. I would be a lot further along in my career and would have had so much more time to help others. Had I received this teaching earlier in life, I would not have done some of the things that I did when I was in the world. I smoked cigarettes from the age of eighteen until I got married at the age of twenty-two. I smoked weed (Marijuana) and drank alcohol from the age of nineteen until twenty-one. I indulged in premarital sex from the age of about nineteen until I married, and I did many other things that were not in God's will. Looking back, I realize that it was all a total waste of my time and money, not to mention dangerous. I knew that when I did those things that it was wrong. I indulged to be social and to fit in. Though my indulgence lasted only a short while, I can now imagine how much more I would have appreciated being a virgin on my wedding day and how much more the Lord would have been pleased with me.

None of the things that I did in my young adult life satisfied me at the time, I always regretted it afterwards. I am sure if you really consider the things that you are doing, you will feel the same way. I tell my husband all the time, "Don't worry about what other people think as long as you know who you are and what you are doing is right." You can't live your life to please other people. Be sure you are pleasing God. If your friends think you are a square, oh well, they don't have the power to put you in hell. It didn't benefit me at the time nor did it benefit my future to appease my friends and family members. My hope is that I can persuade you to take a different route and come to love the Lord before you start indulging in the things that are out of God's will. If you are already indulging in things or a lifestyle that is not conducive to God's Word, it is not too late for you to change. All you have to do is stop and ask God to forgive you, and He will.

I was raised in the church, but I was not taught the word of God correctly and didn't understand any of the Bible. Still today, when I go to visit a church, I hear the same kind of teaching that I heard when I was young. The Old Testament is preached and the old prophets are talked about more than anything else. The New Testament is where life and salvation are and should be preached correctly according to the Apostle's doctrine. I started reading the Bible off and on around nineteen years of age, but I never got any further than Genesis. Being raised in church doesn't make you a Christian or saved. You honestly have to apply yourself and your life to the will of God and have someone who knows the truth of God's word to teach you His will and how to live your life accordingly. I love the Lord and the word of God. It is my life and I pray that I can help someone else find Jesus.

I want you to find Jesus, beloved one. Please don't think that you are too young to devote your life to the Lord. If you are young, strong, and vibrant you are just right for God to use you to influence other young people. You can be so instrumental in saving the lives of so many in the position that you are in. Your friends will listen to you and if you live a godly life in front of them, they will be influenced by you.

Some of you may think that as a teenager even if I had been taught what the will of God was, I still would not have accepted it or lived up to it. I believe that I would have because of the kind of person I am. Once I was taught with understanding, starting at the age of twenty-two, I accepted it. I consider twenty-two years of age to be very young, especially with the mentality of young people today. I believe that young people need Jesus more than ever in this time that we are living in. There is so much going on around you all and so much negativity. There are so many children who have parents that are on drugs and can't care for them. There are so many teenagers having babies that don't know how to care for them or raise them properly. I feel so bad for this generation of children. So, I am soliciting your help. You can be a beacon of light, a positive influence in someone's life.

I hope this scripture will help to encourage you. Had this scripture been brought to my attention, and had I truly understood it, I know that I would have lived my life differently.

Love not the world, neither the things that are in the world. If any man love the world, the love of the Father is not in him. For all that is in the world, the lust of the flesh, and the lust of the eyes, and the pride of life, is not of the Father, but is of the world. And the world passeth away, and the lust thereof: but he that doeth the will of God abideth for ever (1 John 2:15-17).

Now that I understand this scripture I will abide forever, I will do the will of God. I live my life according to the spirit (God) and not the flesh (the world). My soul is precious to me and I am determined that my soul will live in eternal glory. Alcohol, drugs, men, women, sex, money, etc., is not worth eternity in hellfire and damnation. The world, the people in this world without Jesus live for themselves according to their lustful desires and cannot receive Jesus into their lives. But you can!

While loving the world and the things of the world (while lost), I could have died at any moment and would have gone to hell for eternity! You can too, beloved one, please don't allow that to happen to you. You have a greater opportunity than I had. No one taught me the things that I am teaching you right now. All that you have to do is apply this information to your life right now. The things that I did in the world were not worth me going to hell and being out of God's will. And I am sure that if you really think about the things you are doing that are inconsistent with God's Word, you will realize that they are not worth spending eternity in hell either. I don't want any of you to be ignorant of what is expected of you. If you are still breathing and reading this message you still have time to turn your life around for the good. If it were not possible, God would not have said so nor would he have sent his only begotten son to die. He did not need to make a sacrifice for a position that we were already in (lost in sin). He gave His life so that we could live free from sin. All that you have to do is believe that He was, that He is and that He will come again.

I understand how you feel. I know that sin is fun. It's the Devil's job to make it fun and enticing. The Word instructs us to love not the world, neither the things that are in the world. If any man loves the world, the love of the Father is not in him. I've been there, at times it was fun, the problem is that the fun never lasts, and at times it was dangerous to the point that I could have ruined my life. Now I have the love of the Father and I understand that a life outside of God is unacceptable.

Peace of mind is difficult to find or have in this world we live in. I see so many young people including my own children that seem so unhappy, stressed out, depressed, lost, etc., because they are searching for Jesus in all the wrong places; and because they love the world and the things that are in the world instead of loving God who made the world and them. Beloved one, it's not hard nor should you be ashamed to love God.

God would not be God if He did not replace the life that you live now with an even better one once you decided to live for Him. Your peace of mind and health is something that you shouldn't compromise for anyone or anything. You can love and be truly loved by God and your peers if you allow God to live in you. Once you receive God into your heart and start living out His plan that He created you for you will be ever so grateful. When the Holy Spirit comes into you there is no amount of alcohol or drugs that can give you a feeling like Him. Loving God the right way will ensure your safety in this world: The name of the Lord is a strong tower; the righteous run to it and are safe,

Proverbs 18:10. I am paraphrasing, but it is true, we need to seek the safety of the Lord as never before.

When you consider that someone loves you one minute and can turn around the next minute and want to harm or kill you – we need the Lord. With all of the natural disasters and imminent threats that are occurring in the world, we need Jesus. Any disaster or atrocity can happen around us, but If you have Jesus in your life, you will be spared, saved from harm. I have seen it happen and have heard stories of it happening. God protects His people from harm when destruction is all around. I have even been in situations where it could have been me, but bless the Lord oh my soul, He rescued me. He has protected me all of my life, I shouldn't be here nor in the healthy condition that I am in right now. BUT, GOD!

You don't have to feel alone and in despair from day to day. God, the Word of God, is a comfort and a company keeper. Just reading the Word of God can fill your soul with joy. I don't miss anything about the world or the lustful things or people that I engaged with. My life has been filled in every aspect. If I were to die today, I have no complaints. I am forever grateful and I know that it would not have been this way if it had not been for the Lord in my life.

God loves you no matter what you have done or what you are doing in your life right now. He will forgive you of all of your sins. *If we confess our sins, he is faithful and just to forgive us our sins, and to cleanse us from all unrighteousness* (1 John 1:9).

You may think that no one will ever love you or that you can't be loved, that is not true. God loves you no matter what. I love you – that's why I am reaching out to you right now. I want you to be at peace in your mind and live a life full of joy. Satan has taken this world by force. The book of Matthew, Chapter 24 lets us know that time is winding up and Satan knows that too so he is moving rampantly. You don't have to be one of Satan's victims you can be one of God's victors! It's up to you.

I don't pretend to know it all or even a lot, but I do know that the Word of God is true and God is real and that He is coming back one day for His church. I want to be one that He receives into His Kingdom. I pray and hope that you will be one of His Saints also! I cannot say enough that, I love you, and that I want you to be saved from this world of sin and destruction and as the Bible states, *Save yourselves from this untoward generation* (Acts 2:40). We are living in the worst generation of all time: same-sex marriage has been legalized and now marijuana is legal. There is not too much more that Satan can bring to this world that hasn't been done already, just more of it. You don't have to be caught up in all of it, God is a refuge in a time of trouble and present help in a time of need (Psalms 46:1).

I am still a work in progress and will always have room to grow and improve as long as I live, but I am living the life that God desires for all of his creation. The Word of God is inexhaustible, we can read it over and over and still learn something different every time to help us along this journey. Every time I hear my Pastor teach a lesson, I measure myself up to what he is teaching to be sure that I am in line with the Word. It is just a matter of whether you want to live right and then making up your mind to do so. I promise you, living for the Lord is so rewarding on so many levels. God wants His children to be happy and to love His son, Jesus. All of his promises are there waiting for you to receive them. It is God's good pleasure to give us the Kingdom. I implore you, please take control and advantage of your future.

Beloved one, I pray that you believe me when I say

that I love you because I really do! My heart's desire is
that you will understand this message that I am trying
to convey to you because it is a matter of life and death.
I want you to understand how simple it is to just say,
"Yes Lord, I will love you and obey you." The world as
we know it will come to an end one day if we don't leave
it first and I want you to be prepared one way or the
other for your final destination. It doesn't end here. God
is an eternal being and when He breathed the breath of
life into us, we became eternal beings as well. I love you!
But, the real question is: Do you love you? If you do,
please receive my plea to you today and surrender your
all to the Lord. Tell God that you love Him. Thank Him
for His son, Jesus.

As I said, I was a depressed teenager like so many of
you. I would sit on my mother's front porch and think
and pray to God about what I wanted in my future.
Little did I know that God would answer my prayers,
but, He did. Though I was in church and I read the
Bible, I didn't know that I was supposed to love the Lord
with all of my heart and put Him above all else. Thank
God, today I do, and if you will follow these instructions
you will too.

- Bend your knees and ask God for forgiveness
  of your sins, REPENT.
- Read the Bible and go to church and find
  someone that can explain it to you.
- Confess your love to God; recognize Jesus as
  your Lord and Savior.
- Learn to love your neighbor (people) as
  yourself.
- When your spirit starts to convict you for the
  things you do and say, listen to it and stop
  doing it.

- Get baptized in the name of Jesus and walk in the newness of life.

For years I have neglected this responsibility to my family out of fear of the response. I can no longer do that. I can no longer neglect to tell those that are most precious to me that you have to be born again (become a new creature in Christ Jesus) and baptized in the name of Jesus. If you are willing and do these things listed above God will come into your heart and start to change things and people in your life for the better. He is waiting on you beloved one, surrender your all to Him. I love you! I love you with the love of God!

Beloved, let us love one another: for love is of God; and every one that loveth is born of God, and knoweth God. He that loveth not knoweth not God; for God is love. In this was manifested the love of God toward us, because that God sent his only begotten Son into the world, that we might live through him. Herein is love, not that we loved God, but that he loved us, and sent his Son to be the propitiation for our sins. Beloved, if God so loved us, we ought also to love one another. No man hath seen God at any time. If we love one another, God dwelleth in us, and his love is perfected in us (1 John 4:7-12).

Chapter 2

The Holy Bible: Our Life Guide

For our gospel came not unto you in word only, but also in power, and in the Holy Ghost, and in much assurance; as ye know what manner of men we were among you for your sake. **1 Thessalonians 1:5**

The Holy Bible was written for our knowledge and inspiration; for us to know God and develop a personal relationship with him. It is our life guide. It was written in power under the inspiration of God, by the Holy Ghost with much assurance. I haven't found any fault in the word of God. I believe it to be true and necessary for mankind and is incapable of being wrong. There is no other book that you can read that will direct you in this life the way the Holy Bible does unless the context of it was taken from the Bible. Your purpose in life is to do the will of God just as Jesus said was His will and purpose to do. Once we receive the true revelation of the word of God, we can live this life on purpose and with real understanding.

Doing the Father's will – is obeying His word. To obey His word, you have to know His word. Knowing His word helps to establish a relationship with Him. Choose to obey God's word, not man's word and way of life. Man will make allowance for the flesh, but the word of God will deliver you from your troubles and the evils of this world. Peter states, *We ought to obey God rather than men* (Acts 5:29). Obeying God brings peace, deliverance, and power to defeat the enemy. In the Bible when men obeyed God they were blessed, but when they disobeyed God they were cursed. Our inner-man, the soul, lets us know that obeying God is right because when we do wrong our conscience bothers us.

It hurts my heart to hear someone talk against the Bible when it is the unadulterated word of God. I have heard personally and on social media, various ones denounce the word of God/Jesus. It is because they don't know nor understand who God is and don't take the time to read the Bible for themselves. Most people just act on what someone else tells them instead of trying to learn the facts for themselves. I want to try and dispel the notion, the thought, the idea that some of you may have heard that the Holy Bible was written by the white man to control the black man. This is just not true. It's a trick of the enemy, Satan. Please don't just accept what anyone tells you about the Bible or God/Jesus without reading it for yourself.

I don't believe that the Bible was written by the white man to control the black man. God has complete authority over the black man as well as the white man and anything that was ever made was made by Him. Even if it was true, then what the devil meant for bad God has used it for His good. 2 Timothy 3:16-17 declares, *All scripture is given by inspiration of God, and is profitable for doctrine, for reproof, for correction, for instruction in righteousness: That the man of God may be perfect, thoroughly furnished unto all good works.* There is no way that the white man could have written all that is composed in the Bible and not get saved himself; the love of God would have penetrated his heart. You can't read the Bible and not be affected – God's word is too powerful. What is written in the Bible is too magnificent for a mere mortal to have written without the Spirit of God.

Man has created an acronym for BIBLE: Basic Instructions Before Leaving Earth, which makes perfect sense to me because that is exactly what the Bible does. It gives us basic instructions on how to live in this present world and prepares us for the coming of our Lord and Savior, Jesus Christ, and eternal life. Though this definition is not written in the Bible nor stated by God, it is true. The title of the Bible is, "THE HOLY BIBLE." We are supposed to live holy if we live according to the Bible. Most people believe that this is, "The Book." When someone says, "The Bible," it carries the connotation of authority, yet, it is not respected as such.

Most people trust that the Bible is the true word of God. However, most people don't live accordingly nor take advantage of it. We aren't forced to read or live by the Bible that is a choice that we have to make. God was so good to give us basic instructions to live by before leaving this earth we really should take advantage of it. We only get one life to live and we should live it to the best of our ability. According to the dictionary, the Bible is sacred. That part, sacred and holy, is grossly overlooked, but it is there for a reason. God knows that we can live in this present world perfect according to His holy word. Man is the one that says we can't be characterized by perfection nor set apart for the service of God.

I have heard it preached over and over again, that Jesus paid the penalty for our sins and that we can't live perfect or holy; that we just ask God to forgive us and try not to do it again, but that is not what God says in His word. The book of Leviticus 11:44 – 45 states: *For I am the Lord your God: ye shall therefore sanctify yourselves, and ye shall be holy; for I am holy: neither shall ye defile yourselves with any manner of creeping things that creepeth upon the earth. For I am the lord that bringeth you up out of the land of Egypt, to be your God: ye shall there be holy, for I am holy.* God is holy and He requires a holy people. We cannot stand in His presence with the stain of sin in our lives. To sanctify yourself is to set yourself apart from the world–the activities that are worldly and the people that are worldly. You cannot be set apart from the world and yet take part in the things of the world. You are either set apart (sanctified) or (defiled).

Holy does not mean that you don't live life to the best of your ability. God gives you a new way to live that is healthier and more profitable for you. God tells us to be holy as He is holy. Of course, we cannot be just like God, but we can follow the commandments that God has set in place for us otherwise He would not have told us to do so. The ten commandments are just the primary commands for us to live by. The Bible (God's word) gives us many instructions which to live by that are necessary for us to receive salvation and to live this life on purpose. You don't really know what it is to live until you do it God's way.

Our Ministers of today try to keep up with the times and give the people what they want to hear to pacify their souls in order to keep their membership and money. Fear and lack of knowledge prevents them from telling the truth which is going to cause them to enter the lake of fire along with those that follow them. The word of God is clear: Leviticus 19:2 also says, *Speak unto all the congregation of the children of Israel, and say unto them, Ye shall be holy: for I the Lord your God am holy.* You may think this Word only applies to the people of that day, but it applies to us in this day as well, just as much. We are as the children of Israel (when we have chosen to follow Jesus) so this word applies to us when it declares, *Ye shall be holy*. Being holy just simply means obeying the word of God.

Even in the New Testament, it tells us to be holy, Ephesians 1:4 says, *According as he hath chosen us in him before the foundation of the world, that we should be holy and without blame before him in love.* God created us to be a holy being the fall of man doesn't change that, we just have to go about it differently; becoming a new creature in Christ Jesus. And Revelations 22:11 states, *He that is unjust, let him be unjust still: and he which is filthy, let him be filthy still: and he that is righteous, let him be righteous still: and he that is holy, let him be holy still.* All these Scriptures let us know that God requires a holy people. They tell us to be holy as our Father in heaven is holy. Whatever state we are in when we leave this earth: unjust, let him be unjust still: and he which is filthy, let him be filthy still: and he that is righteous, let him be righteous still: and he that is holy, let him be holy still – that is the state that we will die in and will face judgment in.

Ministers of today also say that we can't be perfect: perfect, holy, righteous are all the same, a requirement from God, Himself. Matthew 5:48, supports being perfect: *Be ye therefore perfect, even as your Father which is in heaven is perfect.* And the book of James 1:4 says, *But let patience have her perfect work, that ye may be perfect and entire, wanting nothing.* If God tells us to be holy and perfect without sin, we can do it. If you have the slightest belief that there is a God and that He created all that there is. Then you have to know that there is nothing too hard for Him to do. Allowing you to become holy and perfect according to His standards, separating yourself from the world, is nothing. All it takes is your willingness and determination to do so.

According to God's standard, we are to separate ourselves from the things of this world that are not acceptable unto Him. Man's standard is to party in the night club on Saturday and then go to church on Sunday, or to hate and misuse your brother every day. If we try to be perfect according to man's standard, we will fail. Living perfect according to God's standard is easy, He gives us the help that we need to live up to His standards. Titus 2:11-13 states, *For the grace of God that bringeth salvation hath appeared to all men, Teaching us that, denying ungodliness and worldly lusts, we should live soberly, righteously and godly, in this present world; Looking for that blessed hope, and the glorious appearing of the great God and our Savior Jesus Christ* .... The Holy Spirit is our keeping power and by God's grace, we can be kept. If we allow the Holy Spirit to come in us, it will not only comfort us, but it will convict us when we are tempted by sin and cause us to be strong in the face of the enemy or temptation. If you choose to live for God according to His word in this present world, He will not leave you without the help that you need.

Every aspect of life, every issue that we have in life is expressed in some way in the Holy Bible. Salvation, freedom, marriage, family, children, love, hate, self-fulfillment, sin, life, death, creation, after life, etc., you name it, all answers to life are in there. We all are searching for that something that is going to fulfill us emotionally, that will give us joy and peace of mind. You have to read the Bible to find it. It's the Holy Spirit of God that will give you fulfillment in your mind, body, and soul. You have no real peace until you receive God's Holy Spirit. He is the answer to all of life's sorrows and griefs. The only way to receive God's Holy Spirit is to establish a relationship with God's son Jesus and come to love His word. The only way to establish a relationship with God is to read, accept, and live by the Holy Bible.

God and His word are one, you cannot separate God

from the Word. God is a Spirit; He is not the "man upstairs" or any of the other terms used in reference to Him. Jesus is the Son of God. God sent His Holy Spirit to overshadow Mary the mother of Jesus and His word came alive as His Son, Jesus Christ. *And the word was made flesh and dwelt among us . . .* (John 1:14). Jesus was sent to die as a ransom for our sins and now stands as the intercessor between us and God. The Holy Spirit was sent after Jesus to fill us and provide a way for us not to sin. We have to receive the Holy Spirit before we can have a true relationship with God. *God is a Spirit: and they that worship him must worship him in spirit and in truth* (John 4:24). You can't get the Spirit or the truth except God give it by way of the Word and his Son, Jesus.

You are in error if you put anyone or anything before God. Isaiah 45:18 says, *For thus saith the LORD that created the heavens; God himself that formed the earth and made it; he hath established it, he created it not in vain, he formed it to be inhabited: I am the LORD; and there is none else.* He spoke everything into existence in the beginning. We are the earth that God formed and made by way of the first man Adam and he created the world for us to inhabit it. It seems logical that God would give us the Holy Bible as a roadmap to live by and the intelligence to recognize that we need Him to survive in this world. Without the Spirit of God, we just exist in this life. We have no hope of an eternal future with Him. With the Spirit of God, we live unto Christ who is the author and finisher of our faith and eternal God and Father of us all.

Think about it, if you were to create something wouldn't you want it to do what you created it to do? God is no different. He created us and He wants us to obey Him and live according to the way He has told us to live and to reverence Him as Lord and Master over our lives. Isaiah 45:12 says, *I have made the earth, and created man upon it: I, even my hands, have stretched out the heavens, and all their host have I commanded.* There is no denying, only a God of great power could create this earth and all that dwells in it. And only a great God can love and provide for his creation even when they dishonor and disobey Him. And, yes, He is a good God, Matthew 5:45 states . . . *and sendeth rain on the just and on the unjust.* He is Lord over Heaven and Earth and hell. He is a just God to allow us the necessary comforts of life even when we don't deserve it (the unbelieving and those that dishonor Him). In all of his power, He is yet so loving.

If you are in search of understanding: who you are, why you are here, what it is that you are supposed to do in life; or are just unhappy and need help or answers – I am giving it to you right now. God, Jesus, the Word is your help, your strength, and your salvation. The Holy Bible will guide you through this life and into eternal life with Christ Jesus. Beloved one, you can have the peace and love that you seek and the guidance on your journey through life if you will just believe. Believe that God created you and that he knows the count of every hair on your head. He can and will fix everything that is wrong in your life and give you the assurance that He is with you for all of those things that are out of your control. He wants you to cast your cares upon Him, He cares for you! If you will take the time to read and study the Bible it will change your life and propel you forward to a life that you could have never imagined.

It is better to obey God and live according to His word in order to have a good life and to obtain eternal life. God will not tolerate sin. *Suffer not thy mouth to cause thy flesh to sin; neither say thou before the angel, that it was an error: wherefore should God be angry at thy voice, and destroy the work of thine hands* (Ecclesiastes 5:6). I used to think that God's punishment was too harsh but now that I understand what He has sacrificed for us and how He has made a way for us through His son, Jesus; and the tremendous amount of grace that He has shown us, His punishment is so justified. God is a just and loving God – His mercies are shown upon us every day that we live. If we make the choice to sin in our flesh there lies no excuse when God has proven naturally, spiritually, and physically that He is God.

The grace and mercy of God, His patience, is beyond our comprehension. We are so blessed that God has not destroyed this earth with all of the evil that is displayed before His eyes every day. Many of us discipline our children for their disobedience, God is no different, He will chastise us for our disobedience. We can obey the word of God and live an easy life or we can disobey and live a hard life. *Good understanding giveth favor: but the way of transgressors is hard* (Proverbs 13:15). To get a good understanding of the Word is to obey the Word and receive favor. To learn better is to do better, but, if you do not obey the Word, life is hard. Not understanding life and why you are here keeps you constantly searching for God in all the wrong places.

Depending on your level of faith and how determined you are, it may not be a quick, easy transition into salvation. It's not going to be so easy for you to grasp the Bible all at once. You will have to continue to read, study, and have the revelation of the Word explained to you on a regular basis. I also pray and ask God to open my understanding and reveal the true meaning of his Word to me before I read. I have read the Bible at least 3 or 4 times, maybe even more in the last thirty-seven years, and I continue to find or learn something new that I may have overlooked before or didn't understand at the time. The word of God is inexhaustible. At times it is beautiful, poetic, profound, comforting, assuring, informative, etc. Sometimes the Word of God brings me into submission by reminding me that I am a mere human and that I have to be subject and submissive to a higher power. I have truly had my life questions answered through the knowledge gained from the Bible. The knowledge is free, beloved one, accept it and live.

Reading the Bible for yourself will give you first-hand knowledge of who God is and the validity of His word. If you give the Bible a chance and read it you will see that it is too powerful to deny. The Bible gives mankind structure, rules to live by that creates harmony and peace in your life. It teaches us to love one another to respect each other. How blessed we are to have a look into the future and be able to decide where it is that we want to live forever. We have the opportunity to decide our eternal future. God will always give us what we need to survive in this world, but He will also give us what we want, He's that kind of God. If you want life in Him, He will give it to you, just ask.

Once you start your journey to salvation there are going to be friends or family members that will try and dissuade you. You will need to continue to put your trust in God and constantly remind yourself that there is a higher power and that there is life after death. I have heard that there is no scientific proof that there is a God or that the Bible was written by the prophets with the help of the Holy Spirit. From my perspective, the only proof that anyone needs as evidence of God's existence is to look up and to look around. How does one explain all the things that man could not make: the sky/heavens and all that it encompasses, the weather and the changing of the seasons, the land, seas, and so forth?

Man could not foretell the world's present state as described in the New Testament. Man could not create the foundations by which we humans stand (how we live, think, die, etc.). Man cannot change them, nor can he control them. Man could not create the complexities of the human body. There are many signs and wonders in the world that cannot be explained with the natural mind. God has sent his prophets to explain all of this to us so that we would not be ignorant of his power and grace. The simplest thing that one can do is believe and ask God if He is real and for the revelation of His Word.

Everything around us declares God's glory and majesty. Psalms 19:1-4 is enough to make you believe or to at least think. *The heavens declare the glory of God; and the firmament showeth his handiwork. Day unto day uttereth speech, and night unto night showeth knowledge. There is no speech nor language, where their voice is not heard. Their line is gone out through all the earth, and their words to the end of the world. In them hath he set a tabernacle for the sun.* Praise God! The heavens declare the glory of God! God has made himself known to all mankind. The only effect that man has had on this world is to pollute it with its inventions, thus, the environmental climate change; year-round growth of vegetables and fruit; and cloning of animals, etc. The powers-that-be, have not trusted in God for guidance and its sad to say, but things are not going to get any better, but worse.

It will take faith in God to accept and believe the Bible as truth because the natural mind cannot perceive God's word without faith. As there is no scientific proof to dispel that the Bible is true, there is no scientific proof of time and evolution or how the world was established without a God, only theories. If you can believe what man has written in history and the science books, why not believe the Bible? It makes the most logical sense from Genesis to Revelations. You can't read it like you read any other book. You have to take one Scripture or book at a time and study it more than once. It will amaze you how much knowledge and understanding of life is in it. There is nothing like the anointing/blessing that you receive when reading the word of God and meditating on His goodness.

Jesus tells us to beware of false prophets and some are called wolves in sheep clothing. There are many people that will set examples before you that may seem to make a whole lot of sense, but, don't just listen to what someone tells you even if it sounds convincing. 2 Timothy 2:15 says, *Study to show thyself approved unto God, a workman that needeth not to be ashamed, rightly dividing the word of truth.* If you seek God, He will reveal His truth to you. If you read the Bible from front to back, God's word will prevail. The Scripture says the word of God is a two-edged sword; it will be accomplished in whoever reads it one way or another. It will either cause you to want more and become saved because you understand it and love it, or it will cause you to be convicted in your soul and not want to read it or obey it. Please do not let Satan have that kind of power over your life, you deserve better.

The scripture says that faith cometh by hearing. *So then faith cometh by hearing, and hearing by the word of God* (Romans 10:17). You are hearing the word of God right now, just apply your faith and receive the salvation of the Lord. The Gospel of John 20:30–31 states, *And many other signs truly did Jesus in the presence of his disciples, which are not written in this book: But these are written, that ye might believe that Jesus is the Christ, the Son of God; and that believing ye might have life through his name.* This scripture confirms the Bible was written for us to know and love Jesus, the Son of God, and that we might have life. As you study the Bible you begin to believe in Jesus, the Son of God, and once you believe you will have life eternal. Believing is something that you do, your faith has to be put into action. Your life has to show that you believe and live for God.

I cannot express to you enough that you need to accept Jesus Christ as your personal Savior and turn your life over to Him. It is imperative, literally, a matter of life and death. There is a phrase that states, "I know the Bible is right – somebody's wrong." Don't let that somebody be you. It doesn't have to be you, beloved one. Put your trust in the Lord and in the word of God, the Bible. Other men have come before and other books have been written to prove that Jesus is the Christ, the Son of God and that God is the creator of the universe, but the Bible sums it all up. The Bible has withstood the test of time like no other book in this world. It has gone throughout the world. It has affected more lives than any other book in this world in fact, it is the only book in this world that can give life. God will not be left without a witness. I choose to be that witness today, how about you?

If you should choose not to read beyond this chapter, please take the time to read the four Gospels: Matthew, Mark, Luke, and John in the Bible. They will give you a good understanding of who Jesus is, and will help you to develop a personal relationship with Him. God has chosen to speak and He is working His plan and will complete His plan one day. Any and everything imaginable is happening in the world today. The sovereign God is your only hope. Hear His voice through His word and those that have been sent to teach His word. My true journey began after reading these four gospels. I felt like I really knew who Jesus was (He became a real person to me) and why He was sent to save me (I consider Him to be my personal Savior). I found my reason for living and not being afraid to die, but being willing to die.

The world, meaning the people, are in such a

destructive state, and if this world continues, it is only going to get worse. The three major things that are destroying our young people today: sex, drugs, and homosexuality (LGBT) are taking this world by storm. Marijuana has now been legalized and the law has made allowances for the same sex couples to marry. God is not pleased and He is letting us know it: fires, earthquakes, hurricanes, tornados, cancer, AIDS, etc. Your only escape is through the word of God. Please take heed, we learn and listen to what other people tell us all the time and, in most cases, we believe that it is true, believe this beloved one, the word of God is true. The Holy Bible is the inerrant word of God (that means incapable of being wrong.) Why not believe what is good and will help save your life? You cannot be influenced by the word of God if you do not read it, so please take the time to read the Bible.

These scriptures may give you a little more understanding (God commanded them to write):

- Exodus 34:27 – 28
- Isaiah 30:8 – 9
- Hebrews 2:1 – 4 (God bearing them witness)

The Revelation of Jesus Christ, which God gave unto him, to show unto his servants things which must shortly come to pass; and he sent and signified it by his angel unto his servant John: Whom bare record of the word of God, and of the testimony of Jesus Christ, and of all things that he saw. Blessed is he that readeth, and they that hear the words of this prophecy, and keep those things which are written therein: for the time is at hand." **REVELATION 1:1-3**

Chapter 3

God Loves You More

For God so loved the world, that he gave his only begotten son, that whoever believeth in Him should not perish, but have everlasting life. For God sent not his son into the world to condemn the world; but that the world through Him might be saved. **John 3:16-17**

I hope by now you can feel the love that I have for you. If you can, imagine the love that God and his Son, Jesus has for you. Beloved one, God loves you! There is no other way to say it. Jesus Christ, the Son of God, was sent to us and sacrificed for us because of the great love of God. He was sent because we were lost and without hope. Thank God, he came to save us from this world of destruction, hell, and damnation and to make available to us eternal life. The love of God is obtainable beloved ones, because that's what the great love of God does, the impossible. No matter what you have done God will forgive you. You can question momma's love or daddy's love, but His love for you is irrefutable.

God loved us so much that He came down in a body in the form of His Son, Jesus Christ. God, Himself was the only one that could save us, but He couldn't do it in all of His power – we could not behold His glory.

So, with His power He sent His word, the word of God became the flesh of Jesus Christ. John 1:1-3 says, *In the beginning was the Word, and the Word was with God, and the Word was God. The same was in the beginning with God. All things were made by him; and without him was not anything made that was made.* And John 1:14 says, *And the Word was made flesh, and dwelt among us, and we beheld his glory, the glory as of the only begotten of the Father, full of grace and truth.* The Father/God, the Son/Jesus, and the Holy Spirit/Ghost are all one, yet, they operate separately here on earth. Jesus sits on the right hand of the Father as our mediator between us/man and God. We pray to Jesus and He beseeches the Father on our behalf.

It is imperative that we believe that Jesus is the Son of God. It is through Jesus that God works His plan to save us. We can't get to God except by Jesus. 2 Corinthians 5:18 -19 says, *And all things are of God, who hath reconciled us to himself by Jesus Christ, and hath given to us the ministry of reconciliation; To wit, that God was in Christ, reconciling the world unto himself, not imputing their trespasses unto them; and hath committed unto us the word of reconciliation.* God made a way through Jesus to bring us into relationship with Him. Jesus fulfilled his mission by suffering and dying on the cross for our sins. God in His infinite wisdom and love did this for us, all of mankind. There is no more for Jesus to do to prepare us for the Kingdom, He, himself said, *"It is finished"* (St. John 19:28). The rest is up to us. We have to live life according to His word.

Because we are flesh and blood, God felt it necessary to be a partaker of flesh and blood. The blood of the sacrifice had to be pure so that through death He would destroy the enemy, the devil. *Forasmuch then as the children are partakers of flesh and blood, he also himself likewise took part of the same; that through death he might destroy him that had the power of death that is, the devil*

(Hebrews 2:14). So, He overshadowed Mary, the mother of Jesus who was set aside strictly for this purpose and was a virgin until after Jesus was born, with the Holy Ghost and she conceived a child and called his name, Jesus, the one who would save us from our sins. *And she shall bring forth a son, and thou shalt call his name JESUS: for he shall save his people from their sins* (Matthew 1:21). Prior to the birth of Jesus, we had no escape from sin, but now we can sanctify ourselves by separating from worldly activities/lusts and becoming a new creature in Christ Jesus. *For this is the will of God, even your sanctification, that ye should abstain from fornication: That every one of you should know how to possess his vessel in sanctification and honor; Not in the lust of concupiscence even as the Gentiles which know not God* . . . (1 Thessalonians 4:3-5). We cannot be new in mind and body if we do not separate ourselves from our old ways and way of life. We must abstain from worldly lusts.

Once we sanctify ourselves by turning away from our old ways and bad habits, we become a new creature in Christ Jesus. His death was in vain and a waste to those that don't love Him enough to sanctify themselves. Jesus died so that we could be saved from sin not remain in our sins. Acts 2:38 tells us to, *Repent, and be baptized every one of you in the name of Jesus Christ for the remission (removal) of sins, and ye shall receive the gift of the Holy Ghost.* The Holy Spirit of Jesus will not come into nor dwell in an unclean body/person. True repentance is when one wants to make a complete change in their life allowing the Holy Spirit to come in. Sanctification comes by way of holiness. Holiness comes by way of the Holy Spirit. Holy Spirit comes in by way of separation from sin. *But we are bound to give thanks always to God for you, brethren beloved of the Lord, because God hath from the beginning chosen you to salvation through sanctification of the Spirit and belief of the truth* (2 Thessalonians 2:13). God commands in the Old Testament that we are sanctified. *For I am the Lord your God: ye shall therefore sanctify yourselves, and ye shall be holy; for I am holy* . . . (Leviticus 11:44). There has to be a difference between holy and unholy; between you as a child of God and the life of the world.

Once you come to believe the Scripture and sanctify yourselves as the Scripture has said, you become the beloved of the Lord and then you are free to love Him, free to praise Him, free to receive Him into your heart, and ultimately, free to return to His Kingdom. We are so blessed to have such a God of love who has instilled in us love. Love for one another and love for Him. Yes, it is free beloved ones, it doesn't cost you a dime. God is so worthy of the sacrifice that we have to make of setting ourselves apart from the world. God loves you in all of your sins, but He will not, neither can He, receive you in your sins. You have to clean your mind, body, and heart up before the Holy Ghost will come in and fill your soul. That is your responsibility, set yourself aside from the world and the worldly activities so that God can come in.

God is a Spirit. He is holy and pure. He cannot dwell in an unclean temple, meaning body. If you want Him, you have to make the sacrifice to release all that is not consistent with his Word. This may seem difficult or too much, but it's not. All you have to do is make up your mind to do it. God will strengthen you when you turn to Him. He will feel you drawing near and He will draw nearer to you and send you the help that you need. I have heard too often that, "It doesn't take all of "that" ("that," being: setting yourself aside for the use of the Lord; giving up the world and becoming a new creature in Christ Jesus). *Therefore if any man be in Christ he is a new creature: old things are passed away; behold, all things are become new* (2 Corinthians 5:17). But it does take all of that and more, beloved one. If you are not willing to give up what you know as "your life" and take on a new life in Christ Jesus – you are not worthy of His Holy Spirit. Jesus sacrificed too much for us to do nothing. It took His life – we have to sacrifice our life by giving up the old person that we are and becoming a new creature in Christ Jesus (A person that has changed their whole way of acting and thinking to a person of love and forgiveness.)

We have to love God more than we love ourselves and more than we love anyone or anything. Of course, we can't love God the way we love each other because we cannot see Him. We love Him through His word. The more time that we spend reading and studying His word, the more we come to know Him and to love Him. When you read and understand all the wonderful things that He has done for you and just how much He loves you, you can't help but love Him back. No one knows the mind or the heart of God just as no one can know your mind or heart unless you tell them. We declare our love for one another verbally or in writing, God is no different. He declares His love for us in the writing of the Bible and verbally through His Ministers of the gospel. We have to confess with our mouths that we love God/Jesus and show Him with our lives that we are set apart for his use.

Believe that God loves you, more than you believe when someone else tells you that they love you. When God declares His love for you, He means it. He cannot lie. 1 John 3:1 says, *Behold, what manner of love the Father hath bestowed upon us, that we should be called the sons of God: therefore the world knoweth us not, because it knew him not.* I cannot impress upon you how much love God has for you to make you feel it, but just knowing that God gave His only begotten son for you is enough for you to believe in Him and want to love Him back. By His grace and mercy, God has allowed this sinful world to continue. He is truly a God of love, grace, and mercy. When we love the Lord our God with all of our heart, mind, soul, and strength, we become the sons of God. That makes us heirs to the Kingdom. We become his prince and princesses. We have access to the throne of God.

When we can love Him with all our heart, we have the love of the Father in us. We have an inherent love from birth that God instilled in each of us: love for our mother, love for our father, siblings, friends, mates, etc. That's different from the love that we have to have for our Lord and Savior; we've got to love Him with our whole being, as our creator. God instilled a great desire in us for Him when He breathed the breath of life into man. That is why we get so addicted to so many other things, we are seeking Him. Men and women alike turn to drugs, alcohol, sex, etc., because they can't find that something to satisfy their innermost desire, not knowing or believing that Jesus is the answer to what they seek. We have to spend time with our loved ones to get to know and love them, we have to do the same with God. Reading the Bible, praying to God the Father, and singing songs to the glory and honor of God, helps us develop a relationship with God by which we come to understand and love Him. It's a wonderful life, beloved ones, loving God, Jesus, and having Him love you back.

God created us for Himself – to love Him above all else. We have to choose to love Him, He is not going to force us. We were uniquely created after the image and in the likeness of God. He wants us to come to Him willingly as His created beings. We are an extension of God and having His breath breathed into us automatically give us a portion of His love. We should give that love back to Him. God gave His life for us in the person of His son, Jesus Christ. He didn't have to do that, but because He is such a loving God, He did. We can never thank Him enough for that sacrifice and the only way to repay Him is to give Him what He asks of us, our lives. We expect our children to have some of our character and likeness. We expect them to love us unconditionally. That expectation and desire comes from God. God expects us to exercise a portion of our love and compassion toward Him and toward our brother/neighbor.

When you become a child of God having separated yourself from worldly things, *For ye are all the children of God by faith in Christ Jesus* (Galatians 3:26) and *Wherefore come out from among them, and touch not the unclean thing; and I will receive you, and will be a Father unto you, and ye shall be my sons and daughters, saith the Lord Almighty* (2 Corinthians 6:17-18), receiving the love of God is because you have become blessed, saved, and set apart from the world. *Blessed are they which do hunger and thirst after righteousness: for they shall be filled. Blessed are the merciful: for they shall obtain mercy. Blessed are the pure in heart: for they shall see God. Blessed are the peacemakers; for they shall be called the children of God. Blessed are they which are persecuted for righteousness' sake: for theirs is the kingdom of heaven* (Matthew 5:6-10). This is who you become, beloved one. Your family and friends will no longer know you as the person that you used to be. If you were a person that was sad and had an attitude all the time, that will change. You will become happy and easy to get along with.

When you receive the love or Spirit of God your whole countenance and demeanor changes. You will have joy in your heart and it will show in your countenance. Just as the people of the world don't understand God, your unsaved family and friends will find it difficult to understand your transformation into this new creature in Christ Jesus because they have not yet been transformed. You won't want to go to places such as the night club and hangout with the kind of friends that will keep you from living according to what God has now instilled in your heart. Your language will change. If you used bad language a lot or berated people, you will begin to talk more about God and the love of God and you will show compassion for others. Your thought pattern will change. You will think on good things and your love for God and people; etc. You will have a new and purposeful life! Ephesians 4:23-24 states: *And be renewed in the spirit of your mind. And that ye put on the new man, which after God is created in righteousness and true holiness.* When you become a new creature in Christ you come into your true self and will wonder why it took you so long to live for Jesus. God will give you favor with Him and everyone else in your circle of life.

I regret the time that I wasted giving myself to the world. I could have been so much farther along in my ministry and could have helped so many more people by now. It saddens me when I think about how God could have used me to help change so many lives and all the help that I could have been to the Kingdom. If only I would have had someone to teach me earlier on what it meant to love God and to allow Him to love me. Now that I know, I want to help in any way possible. I hope that I am connecting with your spirit and showing you how great our God is and that He is worthy of your love and to be acknowledged as your Lord and Savior. You have an awesome opportunity to help your loved ones by becoming a vessel for God to use. Learn what is required of you as a new creature in Christ Jesus so that you can show someone else how to come to Christ. My love for God and the Word has caused me to try and redeem my time. Beloved one, don't allow your life to be wasted, just living life. I may not know you, but I love you and I want to help you live your best life possible and that is loving God unconditionally.

You instinctively, know how to love from the Spirit of God which is breathed in you because God is love. You instinctively love your biological family members, but when the unconditional love of God comes into your heart, you can love even your enemies. *But as touching brotherly love ye need not that I write unto you: for ye yourselves are taught of God to love one another* (1 Thessalonians 4:9), *Love you neighbor as yourself* (Mark 12:31); and the Golden Rule as we say, "Do unto others as you would have them do unto you." *Therefore all things whatsoever ye would that men should do to you, do ye even so to them: for this is the law and the prophets* (Matthew 7:12). God loves you, beloved one, He wants you to love yourself and others as He loves. This is one of the major changes that will occur in you as a new creature or child of God. You want to love everybody.

God loves you so much that He has made a way for you to get back to that holy place that Adam and Eve were banished from when they sinned, the peaceable garden of Eden: . . . *and he will make her wilderness like Eden and her desert like the garden of the Lord; joy and gladness shall be found therein, thanksgiving, and the voice of melody* (Isaiah 51:3). We can have that peaceable place in our minds and heart here on earth knowing the great love of God. It changes your whole outlook on life and the way you treat your fellow brother. If God's word was obeyed in this land, we would all love one another and not think evil thoughts or want to cause harm to anyone. The lost state of mankind is all due to the lack of obedience and man's lack of love for God. Following God's law of obedience is a sure way to live a good, peaceful life in this world and the afterworld. That's what this life is supposed to be all about, getting back to the garden of Eden/God.

So many of you are sad and depressed because you don't believe that anyone loves you – God loves you! When you return love to God by being obedient to His Word and loving Him with all of your heart, you will find that you have all that you need in life. God has a unique and unending love for mankind and he wants nothing but the good things of life for us. Jeremiah 29:11 says, *For I know the thoughts that I think toward you, saith the Lord, thoughts of peace, and not of evil, to give you an expected end.* God had a plan when He created mankind and He is working His plan. We have to do our part to fit into His plan and that is to love and obey Him; to understand His word and accept our expected end with Him for eternity. And 29:13 says, *And ye shall seek me, and find me, when ye shall search for me with all your heart.* In order to love the Lord, you have to seek to know Him by studying his word with real intention to understand and build your faith with all your heart. God is just a prayer away. He is not such a high God that you cannot reach Him.

If you are not sure how to show love toward God or anyone for that matter, just start reading the Bible and talking to God. He will listen to you first of all and then He will start to soften your heart toward Him, others, and even yourself. Knowing the good thoughts of peace that God has for you is easy, all you have to do is read the Bible. Changing your mind and opening your heart to receive and believe what God has for you is what most people find difficult to do because most people don't want to give up their life as it is. I implore you, give it a try, surrender your all to God (get on your knees and tell God that you are sorry for all that you have done that wasn't acceptable to Him and tell Him that you love Him and now want to surrender your all to Him). Have faith and see won't God do it for you, He will hear, answer your prayers, and save you. He is an awesome God and He loves you so much! That great love that God has for you causes Him to be longsuffering, He is patiently waiting for you. But He won't wait forever for you to make up your mind. Do it now while you still have time.

What God has asked in exchange for our souls is nothing compared to what our reward in Heaven will be. Of course, we don't deserve all of the chances that God gives us each day we wake up, but God loves us with an everlasting love, Jeremiah 31:3 says, *I have loved thee with an everlasting love: therefore with loving-kindness have I drawn thee.* God loves you and wants you to be saved. God also wants to know that you love Him enough to set yourself aside from the world on your own. God has sent us many signs and wonders (the sun, the moon, the stars, this world, us, etc.) to let us know that He is real and true; all we have to do is look up and see the glory of the Lord! God, in all of His majesty has ways that are beyond our understanding, He has not left Himself without a witness. Nor has He left you without a witness, you see the evil, destruction, and death that reigns in life, you can escape it, beloved one.

Tomorrow is not promised to any of us. People of all ages die every day. We will all die someday. I am so thankful God has given us an escape so we don't have to suffer for eternity, really, just think about it, an eternity of suffering, but then, you have to believe it. Luke 10:21 says, *In that hour Jesus rejoiced in spirit, and said, I thank thee O Father, Lord of heaven and earth, that thou hast hid these things from the wise and prudent, and has revealed them unto babes: even so, Father; for so it seemed good in thy sight.* We have to humble ourselves before the Lord and have the spirit of a little baby ready to receive whatever is required of us through the word of God and say yes to His Word. We can't be like those that are "wise and prudent" not receiving God's word or understanding this life that we live and the fact that one day it will all be over. The revelation of God's word is hidden from those that are too proud to humble themselves down and seek the will of God. But, on the other hand, it is revealed to those that want it and seek for it.

The Word of God is good for your soul, that inner man. Scripture says, *Sweeter also than honey and the honeycomb* (Psalms 19:10). It brings peace in the midst of turmoil. Believing is the principle upon which we are saved because we walk by faith and not by sight. God's love for us is manifested through the sacrifice of Jesus, His Son. Jesus is the way, the truth, and the life. Jesus said to Thomas in John 14:6, *Jesus saith unto him, I am the way, the truth, and the life: no man cometh unto the Father, but by me.* The only way that we can escape death and receive eternal life in Jesus – is through Jesus. Jesus loves us and gave His life willingly for us. We have to give our lives while we live in this present world. Finding the truth of God's word has saved my life and taken me out of the pit of sadness and sorrow, the gloom and doom that this world has to offer. There is a better way to do life, a happier more peaceful way to live this life beloved one, just go for it. Don't worry about the past or the future for that matter, just have faith and live in today believing and trusting God.

Today is all we have we can't control what is going to happen tomorrow. What we can do is purpose in our hearts to get up each day with thanksgiving and praise to God. We have to love Jesus beyond ourselves, our loved ones, and even the world. There is no other way. I have come to the point in my life and with my love for God that I believe if I were to lose my husband or any one of my three children that I will thank God for having them for as long as I have and not turn my back on God or blame Him for taking them away from me. Beloved ones, we have to give God our all and love Him above our parents, siblings, children, spouse, and all others. Love and appreciate God for giving them to us and vise-versa, but, understand that God is the one who blessed us to have them in our lives. Enjoy your loved ones, but put God first in your life. He is the one who gave you life and the one who will sustain your life of peace and happiness.

We have to put life into the proper perspective: God/ Jesus, self, and then our loved ones. Life goes in this order: God/Jesus is the creator, you are the creature, and your loved ones are a blessing to you. When this order of life is disrupted it brings chaos into your life: mental distress, physical illness, destruction, and even death. The Scripture says, *For whatsoever a man soweth that shall he also reap* (Galatians 6:7). It's true, if you don't put forth an honest effort to learn what the will of the Lord is for your life and love Him with all of your heart, you will have a difficult life. God has set in place how we are to live in this world and we can't change that. All we can do is follow his instructions in obedience and love for our ways to be pleasing to Him.

Understand that God loves you above everything else that He has created. His wish for you is that you come to repentance and turn your life back over to Him. He is being ever so patient. His grace and mercy is giving us time and chance upon chance to get it right with Him. Please take advantage of His love and mercy while there is still time. He loves you and has mercy on you whether you are good or bad, in sin or out of sin, whether you love Him or not, He's that kind of God. *That ye may be the children of your Father which is in heaven for he maketh his sun to rise on the evil and on the good, and sendeth rain on the just and on the unjust* (Matthew 5:45). It is His will that no man perish, *The Lord is not slack concerning his promise, as some men count slackness, but is long-suffering to us-ward, not willing that any should perish, but that all should come to repentance* (2 Peter 3:9). Do what you have to do in order to find your way back to God. To perish out of His will is to spend eternity separated from His love.

God loves you beloved one, unconditionally, can you love Him back? I am pleading with you because I love you, but my love is nothing in comparison to the love that God the Father has for you. God knew you before you were conceived in your mother's womb and knows the count of every hair on your head right now. He placed you here for a reason, to give Him glory and to fulfill His purpose for you in this land. Every step that you have taken has been orchestrated by God. You are just as important to Him as the President of the United States or the Pope. If you love Him unconditionally and obey His word, you are even more important to Him. Your reading this book is just another part of His plan – just another stepping stone on your journey through this life. He knew that one day He would send His word to you through me as a reminder of Him, His great love, and to extend you yet another opportunity to love Him.

And we have known and believed the love that God hath to us. God is love; and he that dwelleth in love dwelleth in God, and God in him. 1 John 4:16

Chapter 4

Why You Have Life

For Thus saith the LORD that created the heavens; God himself that formed the earth and made it; he hath established it, he created it not in vain , he formed it to be inhabited: I am the LORD; and there is none else. Isaiah 45:18

Your parents may have stated, "I brought you into this world." That is true. You were conceived and birthed into this world by way of your biological parents. But, make no mistake, God is your creator and sustainer. It is God who established the earth and created man to inhabit it. It is He who has made it possible for you to come here to your parents and by way of your parents. No human can design or create all of the parts and organs that it takes to develop and sustain a human body. Even with the technological advancements of today, man can't keep us alive when God determines our end. It is God that gave you life, and it is God who will determine when your life is no longer needed here on earth.

Sure, medicine and technology have come a long way. There are several ways to conceive a child now, but it is God that gave man the intelligence to be able to do that. Once that seed has been implanted it is still God that causes the egg to develop in his mother's womb into a human being. It is still God who breathes life into the child and causes him/her to become a living soul. Though it has been tried, man can't do what only God can do! I would be afraid to try and do something that only God can do. The first time that was tried hell was created. The next time the language was confounded and men were made to speak in different languages. It is a dangerous thing to allow pride and intelligence to control your position and the place that God put you in as a man. God formed the earth and ALL that is in it, including us.

Man has tried since the beginning of time to change the course of life that God laid out for him, without success. The word of God is the clearest and most logical explanation of our being. Evolution is being taught in the schools, but I won't even entertain the Theory of Evolution. We have life because God gave us life. He breathed eternal life, his Spirit into us. As He cannot die, neither can we except it be His will.

Though Science teaches the religious theory of our being can't be absolutely proven, I beg-to-differ, it is not a theory. There has to be a God to cause everything to be in existence (stars, moon, sun, earth, man, etc.) How intelligence can come from a rock, an animal, and the cosmic theory just makes no sense to me at all. If you take time to read the Bible for yourself God will confirm the truth by His Spirit connecting with your spirit. He will confirm it in your heart and mind that He is real and his word is true. If you pray prior to reading, open your heart, and mind and read with the purpose to understand with God's help, you will. The theory of the Evolutionist absolutely cannot be proven: as far as I know, there is no record of human reproduction via any one of these theories from beginning to end.

Beloved one, it is a matter of life and death that you

come to understand your purpose and life here on earth. Once you die it is too late. I urge you to hear me with your whole being. What I am trying to relay to you is so important. Read and understand the word of God for yourself. God created man in His image and after His likeness to live holy as He is Holy (Genesis 1:26). He will not tolerate any sin in our lives and being a Holy Creator, He shouldn't have to! All you have to do is take heed to His word and live in obedience to His commandants. Satan nor his angels were able to escape the wrath of God once they sinned and neither will we. Hebrews 2:1-3 says, *Therefore we ought to give the more earnest heed to the things which we have heard, lest at any time we should let them slip. For if the word spoken by angels was steadfast, and every transgression and disobedience received a just recompense of reward; How shall we escape, if we neglect so great salvation; which at the first began to be spoken by the Lord, and was confirmed unto us by them that heard him.* How shall we escape? We cannot escape unless we take heed to the word of God. If we neglect the great salvation that has been offered to us, we will deserve the consequences.

Don't continue to live beneath your privilege. If you neglect so great a salvation you will miss out on the promises that God has for you. God has promised that we would become His sons and daughters along with many other promises if we would just live for Him. However, if you disobey His commandments, you will be rewarded with eternal punishment in hell. Give earnest heed to what I am saying to you don't let this message slip from you. Your life is too precious and God is too good and patient with us for us not to take heed to His word. To live a saved life in Jesus is to live the best life that can ever be lived in this world. But you'll never know if you don't give it a chance.

God wants you to trust Him, to cast your cares upon

Him, and to surrender your all to Him. It can be done. All you have to do is humble yourself before the Lord and sincerely repent by asking for forgiveness. He will send His Holy Spirit to help you and keep you from falling back into sin. Ezekiel 36:26-27 says, *A new heart also will I give you, and a new spirit will I put within you: and I will take away the stony heart out of your flesh, and I will give you a heart of flesh. And I will put my spirit within you, and cause you to walk in my statutes, and ye shall keep my judgments, and do them.* Once you receive God's Spirit within, your life will never be the same. You will never view this life the same. You will be new in mind, body, and soul. It will become easy, even a pleasure to obey God's statutes. You become a new creature in Christ Jesus. That's all God is asking of you: that you show Him your love through obedience.

God is our source of life and sustainer of life. He commands our love and obedience, notice that I didn't say demand, He won't force you to love Him or to obey Him. That is still your choice. Matthew 22:37-40 says, *Jesus said unto him, Thou shalt love the Lord thy God with all thy heart, and with all thy soul, and with all thy mind. This is the first and great commandment. And the second is like unto it, Thou shalt love thy neighbor as thyself. On these two commandments hang all the law and the prophets.* This is why you, me, all of mankind, everything, that was created with life was created for God's pleasure and to love God. He created us and then commanded us to love Him.

Love Him with your life: live day by day in honor of Him knowing that He gave you life. When you wake up in the morning, commit yourself to a short prayer to God before you start your day. As you go throughout your day meditate on God, sing spiritual songs in your mind, or out loud, think on good things. Try to find time to read or quote a scripture. Try not to think evil of anyone or do anyone any harm. If you attempt to do this each day – and it will take practice until you can do it routinely – you will do it and before you know it, you will be living daily unto the Lord. Yes, in this present world, it can be done.

I have searched for answers in the natural as to why we are here, but I couldn't find an acceptable answer that would refute the word of God. Let me be specific as to why I believe we have life and what I have found to be true from the Word as to why we were created. Revelation 4:11 says, *Thou are worthy, O Lord to receive glory and honor and power: for thou hast created all things, and for thy pleasure they are and were created.* That includes us, humanity was created to give God the honor and glory with our lives as well as our lips, for He is our Creator. We were created:

- For His joy: to rejoice in Him so that He gets pleasure through our praise and worship.

- For His love: to love Him with all our heart, mind, body, and soul, and to give Him someone to love.

- For His obedience: to obey Him so that He may lead and guide us.

- For His glory: to glorify His name and His Son that He might glory in us.

- For His will: to do His will in accordance with the plan that He has laid out for us.

- For His use: to use us however He sees fit.

I know we shouldn't question God, but, as the saying goes, "I'm human." I wanted to know why I was here on earth and what my purpose is. Not in a curious, unappreciative, nor a derogatory way, but so that I can fulfill my purpose in Him. This is the answer, beloved one, for you as well. We are here to do His good pleasure. *For it is God which worketh in you both to will and to do of his good pleasure* (Philippians 2:13). Life is all good when you live it according to God's good pleasure, His – God's, not ours, but God the Creator.

We can never really know what God was thinking when He said, *Let us make man . . .* (Genesis1:26), other than what the word says. However, we know that He did create us, Genesis 2:7 says, *And the LORD God formed man of the dust of the ground, and breathed into his nostrils the breath of life; and man became a living soul.* We are living and are alive and will never die. We will live forever because God breathed life into us. His Spirit will never die, so we will never die. Our souls will live an eternity either in heaven or hell, no middle ground nor back on this earth to start over. We get this one chance to live for God accordingly and that is it.

We are to live according to how God has instructed us to in the Bible: *And let them have dominion over the fish of the sea, and over the fowl of the air, and over the cattle, and over all the earth, and over every creeping thing that creepeth upon the earth* (Genesis 1:26). This was the original plan for us. Sadly, we have veered so far from it. Which is why I have questions. We, and I say we as humans, have strayed so far from God and holiness that evil is quite prevalent in the land. Having dominion in this world is done with so much pride and self-satisfaction it is nowhere near what God planned for man. Some will kill a human as quickly as they will kill a fly. God is love and he intended for man to rule with love and authority, not pride.

There are five questions that I have asked myself many times and I am sure that you have also. It is important that we answer these questions honestly and completely. These questions, in my opinion, should be answered both naturally and spiritually to be effective.

You have to answer these questions yourself naturally, but I hope that I can shed some light on these questions for you spiritually:

Who am I? What is my identity?

Spiritually, you are a child of God: a Prince or Princess of the King. You are a son or daughter of God. You are a creature that has been uniquely, and "wonderfully made."

(I am a humble servant of the Lord.)

Where am I from? What is my heritage?

Spiritually, you were created by God by way of your forefather Adam and mother Eve. Adam was created from the dust of the ground and Eve was taken from a rib in his side. Then God breathed the breath of life into them, thus, giving you eternal life.

(I am from the earth in which God created me from in the garden of Eden.)

Why am I here? What is my purpose in life?

Spiritually, you are here to give God the glory, honor, and praise; your purpose is to have dominion over the earth and to be fruitful and multiply. God put you here for His use and His pleasure.

(I am here to glorify God in all that I do.)

What can I do?

Decide what you want to do in life or someone else will tell you.

Spiritually, you are to do the will of God and obey God's word. You are to love your brother/neighbor as yourself and do all that you can to help advance the Kingdom of God. Honor God according to His word.

(I can help advance the Kingdom with my knowledge of the Word of God. I can do all things in Christ Jesus because I believe.)

Where am I going? What do you hope for your future?

Spiritually, your hope should be to meet King Jesus one day, preferably, to be lifted up to meet Him in the mid-air with a final destination, Heaven.

(I am determined to go to Heaven to live eternally with my Lord and Savior.)

It's high time for you to know what the will of the Lord is for your life and to live it accordingly. Once you really understand who you are spiritually and what your purpose is in this world, then you can begin to live. God wants you to trust Him and to rely on Him daily for your needs. He wants you to love Him and his Son, Jesus with all your heart. Jesus is now our intercessor, our way to God. We must recognize Jesus as the Son of God and give him reverence as we would give God himself. We pray to Jesus and He hears our prayers and petitions God the Father for us. You are the only one that can answer these questions and make that change for yourself. It's time beloved one!

Jesus is my life: every aspect of my life is affected by Jesus, God, the Word. My past, I look back and see how good God has been to me and I know that I could not have done any of it without Him. My present, I am full with the presence and Spirit of God His peace surrounds me. My future, I look unto Jesus who is the author and finisher of my faith (Hebrews 12:2). I am striving every day to live the best life that I can live in order to make it into the Kingdom of God. Forget about your past, it's gone, you can't get it back. You are responsible for your present, what you do right now will determine your future. Put your future in God's hand, He will direct your path. Whatever you are going through God can handle it. He created you and knows all about you. He will fix it if you ask Him to with a sincere heart. I know, He did it for me and I am no different from you.

I am sure that you have heard many times before that God is a: Savior, Healer, Deliverer, Provider, Father, Mother, etc. He is all of that and more to me. Jesus has blessed me in all of these areas and more. I thank Him daily for allowing me the opportunity to understand and believe in Him. I walk in the presence of the Lord daily and trust in the Lord. I know from experience that there is nothing that He cannot do. I have been healed from several debilitating diseases in my body. I mentioned before about the severe pain that felt like a pinched nerve in my hip and constant back pain causing me to almost not marry my husband. I wanted to be healed of the debilitating pain in my hip. I prayed constantly and though I didn't understand what I read, I read the Bible as often as I could, but, most of all, I believed that God could and would heal me.

Over the past thirty-seven years, I have had several other debilitating diseases/ailments in my body: Ankylosing spondylitis, arthritis in my feet, high blood pressure, a hysterectomy, muscle spasms from my neck to my lower back and chest, and asthma. Through my faith and desire to serve and please the Lord, He has healed me or made it so that I can live with these diseases/ailments and still be the wife and mother that I want to be and even run my own business. I know without a doubt that if I had not found the Lord that I would be in a wheelchair and probably blind by now. I give all honor, praise, and glory, to God for my healings. I know without Him and on my own, I would have given up on being healed.

Now you might ask, why have I had other debilitating ailments if I love and trust God so much? Or, if God is so great why did He allow me to continue to suffer illnesses? Well, if I never had a need for God, I would never know how powerful or good He is. My continued need for God's healing and help keeps me on my knees in prayer and relationship with Him. The same is true for us all, our pain and suffering forces us to call on Jesus and to recognize Him as God in all of his glory and greatness. As long as we live in this sinful world there will be pain, suffering, illness, and death. It's how we endure that makes the difference. If we allow God, He has the power to heal, to minimize the pain, and to bring peace. I also believe that through our trials and tribulations we become stronger and learn who we really are.

Unfortunately, so many of us bow to other gods, people, and things. There are so many people that are depressed and confused about life. So many have committed suicide because they were hopeless and in despair. Beloved one, you don't have to be one of those people. God is your answer to life and a more abundant life, (St. John 10:10). The mistake that we make is that we try to please ourselves in this life. We were created for God's pleasure not our own. If you please God first, *Seek ye first the Kingdom of God* (Matthew 6:33) and *And He shall give you the desires of your heart* (Psalms 37:4). Obey his commandments and God will bless you to receive all of the good things in life. You don't have to work so hard to be happy or to accomplish so much in life. All it takes beloved one, is a true dedicated life in Jesus.

Thou art worthy, O Lord, to receive glory and honor and power: for thou hast created all things, and for thy pleasure they are and were created. **Revelation 4:11**

Chapter 5

The Newness of Life

What I understand of the people of today is that the majority are caught up in the world and worldly activities. There is no regard for God, Jesus, the Lord, or the Holy Spirit. It has been proven time and time again that people of today don't even have sufficient regard for their own lives much less anyone else. Sometimes I feel that we are back in the wild west days where you could just walk up to someone and shoot them, and then take what you want from them. The god of this world – Satan – has deceived the minds and hearts of the people in a big way. But more than that, prophecy is being fulfilled: the signs of the end of time are prevalent and have been for years.

You may have heard it said for years, but rest assure, one day it will be fulfilled sooner than we think: the return of the Lord. The main prophecy being fulfilled is, *Wars and rumors of wars* . . . (Matthew 24). We hear of talk of war on the news every day. Someone is killed or dies every day. There is no peace to be found in this world without God. The minds and the hearts of people are only going to get worse and our only hope is that we individually get better by receiving the Lord, Jesus. Possessing the Spirit of God will give you the peace you need to feel safe. It will give you the joy you need to keep going each day, and it will secure a place for you in heaven.

You have the power to change your circumstances, your surroundings, your thinking, your behaviors, whatever it is in your life that is preventing you from developing a true relationship with God. All that the world has to offer you is death, destruction, pain, and sadness. I am proposing a better way of life to you. All it requires is that you believe to the point of conversion into a new creature in Christ. Beloved one, you won't miss out on anything or any pleasure that you think you need now. God wouldn't be God if he couldn't or didn't replace your needs and desires with other more blessed needs and desires. I know because I felt the same way when I was young. I didn't think that it was necessary to give up all the pleasure that I enjoyed in my old life. but it was. You can't straddle the fence, so-to-speak. You can't serve God and the Devil at the same time, it is one or the other.

I can't express to you in words how much you need the Lord, Jesus Christ. The Devil is real and he knows that his time is short. Satan is destroying the minds of young people and making them believe that they can do whatever it is that they want to do in this life contrary to God's command. God is trying to get your attention every day. Death and destruction are all around you. I see how negativity is affecting you with sadness, depression, feeling and looking lost, anxiety, even the contemplation of suicide. Beloved one, you can be happy and have totally the opposite outlook on life when you make up your mind to walk in the newness of life with Christ Jesus. I promise, walking with Christ Jesus will empower you.

There is more to being saved and being a Christian than most think. We can't do it casually but, it is not hard to do either. It just takes making up your mind and doing it. God has a standard that he wants his people to live by, so does Satan. God's standard is that you be a respectable, loving, kind person, that you love your neighbor as yourself, that you do to others as you would have them to do to you, and that you give reverence and praise to Him. Through God's standards you find and understand God's goodness and the goodness in life. Living by Satan's standards will leave you in constant disillusion, depression, oppression, and without hope.

Beloved ones, don't be deceived, you can't just confess with your mouth that you accept Jesus into your life and continue to live the same way that you have always lived. Jesus had to take on the sins of the world and shed his blood so that we might be saved. That is a huge commission so we have to make a sacrifice as well. We have to crucify this old man (our flesh) and walk in the newness of life in Christ Jesus. 2 Corinthians 5:17 says, *Therefore if any man be in Christ, he is a new creature: old things are passed away; behold, all things are become new.* Once we take on the Lord, Jesus Christ, all things become new in our lives. We have a new way of thinking, a new walk/places that we go, new talk/confessing the Lord Jesus etc. To be saved and walking in the newness of life is to change your whole direction in life and set yourself apart from the world and aside for the use of the Lord.

One thing that isn't talked about much, especially in the church, but has been in the news lately is suicide. I have heard several testimonies recently from young people that have contemplated it. One of the Ten Commandments specifically states that, *Thou shalt not kill* (Exodus 20:13). That includes yourself. If you commit suicide you have killed yourself. If you kill yourself you are dead and cannot ask God for forgiveness. Please don't take this route to solve your problems. It only serves to multiply your problems beyond your human imagination for an eternity. Think about all of the loved ones that you will leave behind to deal with your loss. Try God. If you can't see any other way out and have exhausted all measures that you are capable of, then please, try God. Pray to Him and ask Him to help you. Put it all in His hands. He knows all about you and your troubles. He is just waiting on you to release it to Him so that he can heal you. He will give you the hope and assurance that you need to save your life.

Trust Jesus, if you have tried it your way and have not been successful. Decide in your heart that you want to change your life and become a new person in Jesus Christ. God will cause your whole life to change for the better and for the good. It is possible beloved one! All it takes is faith and your honest desire to change and live for Jesus. I have seen this happen many times. One person that I know lived in the streets and was on drugs for many years, in and out of jail. He made up in his mind that he was tired of living that way and came to Christ. He is living a life now that was unimaginable before he converted. He is able to testify to other individuals who are living unsaved and help them change their lives.

I have to be specific in telling you the truth. You have to live according to how God has instructed us to live in His word, by His commands. It all may sound too difficult or too much in the beginning but, most things worth having in life are difficult in the beginning. Anything in life worth having comes at a price, but the ultimate price you will have to pay is sacrificing the old you. New life is yours for the asking, beloved one. Pray right now, "Lord I commit my life to you, mind, body, and soul. Please come into my life and heal my mind;

please deliver my soul and free me to live peaceable in this life and restore my soul." He will do it!

Listed below are just some of the things that you have to stop doing in order for you to receive the Holy Spirit and allow God to come into your life. Most people fall into one or more categories. You can't have a true relationship with God in your present state if you take part in any one of the following and II Corinthians 7:11 says, *Having therefore these promises, dearly beloved, let us cleanse ourselves from all filthiness of the flesh and spirit, perfecting holiness in the fear of God.* The Bible does not specifically say what filthiness of the flesh is, but, the things listed below are contrary to God's law and society (man's law) and must be eradicated for you to live a life in Jesus. Sex, drugs, and money are the three biggest obstacles preventing one from walking in the newness of life. I have not listed these in any particular order and some may seem to be nothing to some of you, but it does have an effect on your salvation and how God perceives you as His son or daughter.

Fornication (pre-marital sex): Waiting for marriage to have sex may sound like a foreign concept today. Most people are astonished or shocked to hear someone say that they are waiting for marriage to enjoy sex. So many children are born out of wedlock now, that it is not a big deal anymore. Children are raising themselves, or being reared by grandparents because the one parent that they do have has to work, or is too irresponsible to care for them. God ordained marriage for man and woman, and sex was intended to come after marriage for procreation not the pleasure that is sought for in sex today. The one you join your body to is supposed to be your soulmate. There is no need to "test the waters" or as I have heard said, "I need to know what I am getting before we get married." If you allow God to send you your mate and you allow God to create in you a new heart, He will bless you with just what you need in a life partner.

Adultery: Men and women are committing adultery as if they never took vows to love one another until death do them part. When marriage gets hard the vows are forgotten and disrespected. Marriage is to be honored. Man is to love his wife as Christ loved the church and gave his life for it. The wife is to honor and obey her husband and to respect him. Marriage is a frame of mind, and you have to decide that you are going to honor your vows and make it work with the one that you have committed yourself to. Pride is what destroys the marriage. Once you have argued so long and disrespected each other so many times you just want to give up on the marriage and start over with someone else. If you can make it work with someone else you can make it work with the one that you have taken vows to love and honor until death do you part. Release your pride, humble yourself and forgive. We as men and women are all made the same and have all of the same body parts. What you do with someone new you can do with the one that you are already with. Compromise with each other, love and respect each other and seek the Lord and counseling.

Lying: The scripture says, . . . *and all liars, shall have their part in the lake which burneth with fire* (Revelation 21:8). God cannot stand liars. They will not be able to tarry in His sight. However, most human beings lie. Without the Holy Spirit to convict you, lying is almost an automatic thing to do. You end up telling one lie after another, and pretty soon you don't know what truth is. God hates liars because He is truth and cannot lie. We were born into sin, so lying comes to us without practice or training. Lying is unacceptable to God and it ends up hurting more than helping. When we receive salvation and become a new creature in Christ Jesus, we receive a new tongue, we not only praise Jesus, but we also stop lying. Scripture also says, *The tongue is the hardest thing to tame* (James 3:8-14), but it can be tamed when we are converted into a new creature through Christ Jesus.

Family Curses: You don't have to follow in the footsteps of your family or forefathers. You can break any curse that has been upon your family, regardless of how many generations your family has been controlled by it. Just because your mother or father did it, whatever it is, doesn't mean you have to do it or be that way. Becoming a new creature in Christ Jesus means that you become a totally new person. Those old ways and old ways of thinking are passed away. You can rise up to be a new example for your family and for those loved ones who come after you. Some families have been cursed or plagued with certain health issues, mental issues, alcoholism, drug addictions, rapists, victims of rape, pornography, murderers, the list goes on. You don't have to be any of those things or have any of those illnesses. Jesus gave us a way out. Through prayer and believing in Jesus, you can prevail and live a victorious life.

Profanity: Everywhere I go, and on social media, I hear and see profane words – a total disregard for people that should be respected: children, elderly, parents, clergy, etc. You disrespect yourself when you use such language. It makes you look ugly, and not as cool as you may think. It sounds so horrible to hear young people, both male and female, talk this way. It is even more unbecoming for a woman to use profanity. Why use profanity? It doesn't make you grown. It doesn't make the opposite sex want to get with you – as the young people say. It doesn't make you sound intelligent, just the opposite. Using profanity is a way to fit in with your peers and make you sound cool.

You should be less concerned with what your peers think or say. Fear God above all else and everyone else. Scripture instructs us not to allow filthy communication to proceed out of our mouths (Colossians 3:8). It is a disgrace to God, especially when you use His name in vain. He is holy and wants nothing but holy, righteous, conversation coming out of your mouth, praises unto him and kindness toward your fellowman.

Alcohol, Drugs & Smoking/Vaping: It is a proven fact these all destroy the body and the mind rather legal or not. Why would you ingest something into your body that destroys your mind and body? Why waste your money on something that is going to send you to an early grave? The rate at which cancer is killing people these days should be a major deterrent, in addition to the high price tag. Alcohol and drugs are dangerous and place you in precarious situations. They are also very addictive. You may think it won't happen to you, but you don't know how your body and mind will respond to alcohol and drugs. You may become immediately addicted. You also will not know what substances are mixed into the drugs you are ingesting unless you prepared it yourself. There have been many people who thought they were taking one thing and ended up ingesting something that drove them out of their minds. Trying to be cool like your peers is not worth losing everything and everyone which is what happens when you succumb to drugs and alcohol or when you are diagnosed with cancer after smoking for years. Headlines are becoming common of teenagers dying from the chemical changes associated with THC and vaping.

Clubbing/Partying/Hanging Out: Most times when people go out clubbing it is because they want to meet someone, either for a one-night hookup, or for starting a lasting relationship. If you just want to hook up for the night, then the club or party is the right place. However, if you are looking for your life-long partner, the club is not the place to find him or her. I know because I did it too. What a waste of my time. I found my beloved in church after I prayed to God to send the right man. Pray and wait on God to send you the person that He wants you to join in union with. Two major problems with partying, are the way women dress to gain the attention of men and how women allow men to dance with them. It is so disrespectful! Please, take some pride in yourself and dress as becoming a lady and refuse to allow men to rub their bodies all on you when dancing. They are not your husbands and they have no business fondling your body. When you shake your booty – twerking as they say – all over the dance floor for them to see you is also a disrespect to yourself and gives them the green light to disrespect you. Ladies, if this is your behavior, the men are not going to take you home to meet their mother nor "put a ring on it". As for the guys, why do you treat women like they are less than mothers, sisters, wives, daughters? There are special women in your life that you would not want to see treated this way. So, why do you treat other females with less respect than you want to be extended to the women in your life? Men, women are looking for someone that they can take home to meet their fathers. Not, a man that is going to disrespect them on the dance floor the first time you meet them.

Disrespect & Disrespecting Women: There is a lot to be said on this matter, but I will be brief. Women, please, respect yourselves enough to not allow anyone to disrespect you in how they treat you, misuse you, or abuse you. God loves you no matter who you are, where you came from, or what you look like. You have to love yourself enough to demand respect. Men, if you love yourselves and allow God to come into your heart, you won't have the desire to disrespect or misuse women. When you have a constant need to disrespect others, it is because you are lacking something in yourself. God can fill that void if you will allow Him. We should treat everyone the way we want to be treated. God did not create males or females to be doormats or punching bags. The Word of God states that we are wonderfully and beautifully made. We must believe that and demand to be treated as such.

Cohabitating: Living together outside of marriage is a common practice in today's society. God did not tell us to do a trial run before marriage. Living under the same roof with the opposite sex as if you are married is unacceptable to God. You are playing house. You should have enough confidence in who you are to know if you are ready to share your life with someone else in marriage. If you are not sure, you should wait until you are. You are setting yourself up for failure and telling that other person that you don't feel worthy of a permanent commitment. To love someone is to respect them, and to put their best interest above your own. Living together for financial convenience is not acceptable either. It turns into "friends with benefits" or it negatively impacts the relationship. Cohabitating displays a lack of trust. God says, *Marriage is honorable among all, and the bed undefiled; but fornicators and adulterers God will judge* (Hebrews 13:4). The union of a man and a woman was instituted in reference to the church. Metaphorically, we are the bride of Christ and marriage should be honored as such.

Disobedience to Parents: The first commandment with a promise is: *Children, obey your parent's in the Lord, for this is right. Honor your father and mother which is the first commandment with a promise. So that it may go well with you and that you may enjoy long life on the earth* (Ephesian 6:1-3). Unfortunately, this is not always the case with so many. Children of all ages, from their youth to adulthood, routinely disrespect and disobey their parents. If you can't obey your own parents, you are going to have issues with anyone in authority. Disrespecting and disregarding authority could land you in jail, or worse. Having no respect for the people that brought you into this world, means no respect for yourself or anyone else. Disrespect is a learned behavior, due mostly to what is tolerated by the parent(s) raising the child. Once you become of age and know right from wrong, you are accountable for how you treat your parents and elders. Your parent(s) could be wrong in something that they say or do, but you are not to challenge them or go toe-to-toe with them in an argument. It is better to walk away. The time will come for you to express yourself in a respectful manner. God will bless you for your obedience and humility. My husband and I are blessed because neither of us has ever argued with our parents. I will acquiesce when I see that my point of view is not being accepted by my mother. By doing so, I have established a good relationship with my mother.

Disgraceful Dress Code: Just as females should not expose their undergarments to the viewing public, young men should not wear styles that display their underwear or buttocks. Contrary to popular belief, the general public is offended by your visual display. Everybody would think that I had lost my mind if I were to walk down the street with my pants on my thighs and my panties exposed, or some would think that I was a prostitute. It is no different with a man. You are disrespecting women and yourselves when you dress in this manner. The style may give you a sense of being, or an air of toughness, but it can also hinder your progress in life as this attire is unacceptable in the workplace. To be a respected man is to behave in a manner that demands respect from your peers.

Relationship Merry-Go-Round: Going from one relationship to another because things didn't work out is not God's way. You should not enter a relationship with anyone until you have observed that person over a period of time to see if they have respect for themselves and others. Do they have a relationship with God? What are their goals? Only after marriage, should the relationship turn physical. Any sexual activity before marriage is fornication. I know this is not something that is done anymore, but if you want your life to be pleasing to the Lord, you must commit to God's way. Why continue to get your heart broken time after time, entering one relationship after another, compromising more of yourself than you want to or should? Allow God to send you your mate, and it will last a lifetime. Each time that you enter a relationship that doesn't work out, you lose a piece of yourself. Saving yourself for that one love is far better. When you join with your soulmate, the passion is much deeper and the intimacy, worth waiting for!

Internet Porn, FaceTime Exposure & Phone Sex: Young people are being exposed too early to these disgraceful activities. In the home, at school, on social media, it's everywhere. Sex is no longer just an adult activity. Once you expose yourself over the Internet or over the phone via text messages, it's there for the whole world to see if someone wants to expose you or it. Just in case you haven't heard it before, **ORAL SEX IS SEX.** And it is happening in schools, at parties, in the clubs, behind the church building, anywhere and everywhere. I encourage you to stand up and stand strong against peer pressure. Don't allow yourself to be taken advantage of this way. Say, "NO!" You don't have to participate in this behavior to be cool or accepted.

Seek the advice of a trusted adult, or your Physician before consenting to this behavior. It can have severe, life-long consequences. The internet definitely has its advantages, but it can also yield disastrous results. It is a trick of the enemy – the devil – to depend on the internet for friends and validation. Don't be deceived, once you have indulged in this type of behavior you can't get your innocence back. Be wise, learn how to protect yourself and don't feel like less of a person if you choose not to indulge in sexual activity until you are married.

Pornography: I listed this separately because it is mostly indulged in by males. Pornography is unacceptable in God's sight. It is still sin to lust after a woman whether you physically touch her or not. If you are married and lust after a woman other than your wife, be it in person, in a magazine, on the internet, or a movie, you are committing adultery. Jesus said, *But I say unto you, That whosoever looketh on a woman to lust after her hath committed adultery with her already in his heart* (Matthew 5:28). So young men, you are committing adultery according to God and he is not pleased with your behavior. This is also true for women indulging in pornography.

Homosexuality/Lesbianism/Transgender: Society has strayed so far from God's law that laws now make same-sex marriage acceptable. Homosexuality is common in all social circles. Despite what society and the government allows, it is still sin in God's sight. In the Bible, the two cities of Sodom and Gomorrah were destroyed by God as a punishment for the wickedness of their inhabitants (desiring a person of the same sex to lie with in a sexual manner). It is so widely accepted in today's society, that our children are learning about "alternate lifestyles" in elementary schools. Our future generations are being inundated visually and verbally with same-sex orientation. *You have the right to love whoever you want*, is being taught throughout the land. Children these days don't have much of a chance without the teaching of God's word.

I understand that we are dealing with Millennials and Generation Z, but God is still the same. He has not changed. Therefore, his law has not changed. If you are caught up in this philosophy, you can change your way of thinking. When you become a new creature in Christ Jesus, old things will pass away, including your abominable, sexual sins. *If a man also lie with mankind, as he lieth with a woman, both of them have committed an abomination: they shall surely be put to death; their blood shall be upon them* (Leviticus 20:13).

You can continue to believe what society says, you can even hate me for speaking against it, but it won't change the fact that God has the last say and He will judge accordingly. Same-sex relationships are considered inordinate (unconscionable, immoral, appalling) affection in God's sight. *Mortify therefore your members which are upon the earth; fornication, uncleanness, inordinate affection, ...* (Colossians 3:5). Those are strong words, but He wants you to understand how much He is against this type of behavior.

Idol Worship: Worshiping anyone or anything other than the true and living God is sin. We are to love the Lord God with all of our hearts, minds, bodies, and souls. Why would you worship something or someone that can't save your soul? Someone who can't be a present help in the time of need? Worshiping famous people and spending your time and money following famous people is a waste of time. Think about it, if you need them, are they going to come to your rescue? Are they going to even acknowledge your existence? I choose to worship the one who has all power in His hands and has sacrificed His life for me. The one who is a present help in the time of need. I can call on Him any time of the day or night.

To recap, you have got to come correct with God. You can't disobey God's word and change the life plan that God has laid out for you. God created us to lie with the opposite sex only within the confines of marriage. Getting high and drinking with your friends or indulging in things because it makes you feel grown or you are trying to fit in with your peers, puts you in danger and alters your mind with substances that aren't supposed to be in your body. It's all unacceptable in God's sight. Young men, please pull your pants up, put a belt on and present yourself in a respectable manner, so that life can present better opportunities for your future.

God has a far greater plan for you. All you have to do is receive it. What you are seeking in things will not make you happy. Things are only temporary and don't provide any real joy. Only God can give you the real joy that you are seeking. I beseech you, beloved ones, let it all go and give God a chance – walk in the newness of life. When you walk in the newness of life, you get a taste of heaven here on earth. Of course, we will make mistakes, we are human. God simply asks that we obey him and love him with all of our hearts. Once you come to the frame of mind to give God your all, you won't have a desire for all of those other things. Then, you will be found of Him in peace, without spot, and blameless. Give this new life a chance, I promise, you won't regret it.

Mortify therefore your members which are upon the earth; fornication, uncleanness, inordinate affection, evil concupiscence, and covetousness, which is idolatry: For which things' sake the wrath of God cometh on the children of disobedience. **Colossians 3:5-6**

Chapter 6

Your Soul Will Not Die

It is my duty as a born-again believer to tell you what I have learned of God and of His word. As the Apostle Paul, I am, *Holding forth the word of life; that I may rejoice in the day of Christ, that I have not run in vain, neither labored in vain* (Philippians 2:16). It gives me joy in my heart and great pleasure that I can tell you of the goodness of God. I know that my labor on your behalf will not be in vain because I am holding forth and proclaiming the word of God. I am running this race to the Promised Land as fast and as best as I know how. All I want to do is encourage you to come along with me. You see when you love the Lord as much as I do and come to understand his Word, you cannot keep it to yourself. You want everyone that you know and love to be saved and prepared to go back with the Lord when he comes.

I thank God that even after Jesus shed his blood, we still have to make sacrifices in an effort to do our part to make it into the Kingdom. If God would have allowed the shedding of Jesus' blood to have completely removed the stain of sin from humanity without us having to do our part of separating from the world (sanctifying ourselves), how would God know that we loved Him? This world would not be worth living in. Imagine the constant pandemonium that would be in this world without the Holy Spirit to govern those that are godly. If I am wrong, I will go to Heaven either way, but, if you won't believe and make a change in your life, you lose. You will go to hell when you die. I implore you, please hear with your ear and let it go deep down into your heart.

Despite what you believe or have been taught, there is no escaping hell if you do not obey God's word to live free from sin. God's word is true. He has spoken it, and it will come to pass. There are many theories as to where we go when we leave this earth. You may even question if we have a soul that will live for an eternity. The truth is exemplified in the word of God, the Bible. Genesis 2:7 says, *And the Lord God formed man of the dust of the ground, and breathed into his nostrils the breath of life; and man became a living soul.* Meaning: God put his Spirit inside of us and that created an eternal spirit man (a soul) in us that will never die. God gave us life from His breath and we became a living soul. So, as God will never die neither will we. Our physical body will return to dust (Ecclesiastes 3:20), but our spirit will live forever.

Humanity has come to understand the living soul as possessing life. Living is eternal. How you live on Earth, is how you will live in eternity. If you live for Satan on Earth, you live for Satan for eternity. You have the choice to live for God now, and for eternity. You can live now, with the Holy Spirit guiding you in this world by the word and faith into eternal life in Jesus or you can ignore it and continue to live in this world by your own knowledge and lead yourself into eternal damnation.

I believe with all of my being that God's word is true and forever settled in heaven. Psalms 119:89 says, *"Forever, O Lord, thy word is settled in heaven."* My faith in God was sealed the moment I heard my Bishop read this scripture. His word is even above His name, Jesus (Psalms 138:20). As the Spirit confirmed for me that His word was true, I knew that He would fill me with His Spirit and honor His promise to me of eternal life in Him. I have relied on comfort from the Holy Spirit every day of my life since, and He has not steered me wrong.

There are many philosophies on life after death. However, the Bible is your greatest source of information regarding this life and the afterlife. It is your responsibility to search the scriptures and learn what is true. I believe there is life after natural death. I am not afraid to die. I know that if I continue to live a pleasing life before the Lord that I will spend eternity with Him in his Kingdom.

Beloved one, life consists of: being born (by way of another human; a woman), living on earth for a period of time (in which we are to be converted and become new creatures in Christ), and dying (after which we live for an eternity). Our soul that governs our behavior will never die. The physical body will perish. God is our Creator and he created us to live for him. Originally, to live in the Garden of Eden as Adam and Eve did. Unfortunately, Satan came into the Garden and deceived Eve and here we are. God's great love made a way for us to get back to that garden (Heaven) through the sacrifice of His Son, Jesus Christ.

The shedding of Jesus' blood provided us with a way back to Heaven. Salvation is free, all we have to do is surrender to God's will. We are saved by grace, through faith, believing is the principal application of sanctification. Isaiah 55:1-3 demonstrates how free and available salvation is. *Ho, every one that thirsteth, come ye to the waters, and he that hath no money; come ye, buy, and eat; yea, come, buy wine and milk without money and without price. Wherefore do ye spend money for that which is not bread? And your labor for that which satisfieth not? Hearken diligently unto me, and eat ye that which is good, and let your soul delight itself in fatness. Incline your ear, and come unto me: hear, and your soul shall live; and I will make an everlasting covenant with you, even the sure mercies of David.* The Word of God is good. Let your soul delight itself in fatness and fully indulge yourself in God and His word. Buying wine and milk is referring to you diligently seeking the truth of the Word of God. Delve into it. Seek the revelation of God's word, it is life for you. If you take heed to what I am saying and obey God's word your soul will live. This is God's promise to us.

Please don't just sit in church and listen to the Preacher. "Go home and read the Bible for yourself. Search the Scriptures in them you will find life," is what my Bishop would say. Start with the 4 gospels: Matthew, Mark, Luke, and John. Those books will give you a good idea of who Jesus is, and will help build your trust in Him. If you are going through something right now, read the book of Psalmss, it will give you much comfort. Isaiah warns the men of Jerusalem to hear his words, and so I warn you, hear and listen carefully to what the Word is saying to you and your soul will live in heaven for eternity (Isaiah 28:23).

Pray and ask God to direct you to a Pastor who can teach you the truth and help prepare your soul. It is so important to have someone teach you that has a revelation of God's word and not opinion. A true teacher of God's Word can open your understanding. A true teacher will tell you once our physical body ceases to function, our spirit will live eternally. You may have seen this depicted in movies, or have heard different ones talk about their experience of dying and walking toward the light. It has been so good of God to give us ways and examples of life here on earth and life after we leave this earth so that we know what to expect. He has not left Himself without a witness nor has He left us without an escape. Jesus, himself, was raised from the dead after the third day and is now seated on the right hand of God (Mark 16:19). Read it for yourself. The Word of God speaks for itself.

Beloved one, there is too much information included in the Bible that lets you know that you need to prepare yourself for the second coming of Jesus Christ. Please understand, that it won't be long before He returns. You need to prepare your mind, body, and spirit for His return so your soul will be caught up to meet him, not cast down into hell for eternity. Jesus is not coming to set up another kingdom here on earth to allow you another chance.

God gave us a way to go back with him, to heaven, to live in eternal peace. That was the original plan before Satan deceived Eve. I Peter 5:10-11 says, *But the God of all grace, who hath called us unto his eternal glory by Christ Jesus, after that ye have suffered a while, make you perfect, stablish, strengthen, settle you. To him be glory and dominion for ever and ever. Amen.* Through the shedding of Jesus' blood, we have a way back to glory. Notice the scripture says, *who hath called us unto His eternal glory.* God is eternal and so are we. Our souls will never die. You have the choice of allowing God to make you perfect, stablished, strengthened, and settled, in heaven. I am looking forward to being out of this world of suffering and in heaven so I can give God glory forever and ever. Eternity is a long time – beyond our imaginations, but I can imagine what hell must feel like and I want no part of it.

I know Jesus as my personal Savior. I have studied the Bible for myself and practiced Christianity for the past thirty-seven years, so I feel that I am qualified to speak what I know on God's behalf. John 14:17 says, *Even the Spirit of truth, whom the world cannot receive, because it seeth him not, neither knoweth him: but ye know him: for he dewlleth with you, and shall be in you.* I am speaking truth and I have lived my life so that I know that I have the Spirit of truth dwelling in me. This may sound foreign to you right now, or a bit confusing, but the more you read the Bible and are taught the true word of God, the easier it will be for you to understand the message I am trying to convey.

I follow the Apostle's doctrine, the old path, the only way to find the truth. The Apostles continued with the inerrant teachings of Jesus Christ, Himself the inerrant Word of God. The Apostle's doctrine emphasizes repentance for the remission of sins, love for one another, and admonishes husbands and wives to love and honor each other as Christ loves the church. For us to choose good over evil. The doctrine also teaches us to love the Lord our God with all our hearts, minds, bodies, souls, and strength, to baptize in the Name of Jesus and so many other commandments or laws that have fallen by the wayside due to the lack of true revelation. If we neglect to follow the Apostle's doctrine, we will spend eternity in hell, fire, and damnation. According to John the Revelator, *And whosoever was not found written in the book of life was cast into the lake of fire* (Revelation 20:15). Be sure your name is written in the book of life, by obeying the Word of God.

If ye then be risen with Christ, seek those things which are above, where Christ sitteth on the right hand of God. Set your affection on things above, not on things on the earth. For ye are dead, and your life is hid with Christ in God. When Christ, who is our life, shall appear, then shall ye also appear with him in glory. Colossians 3:1-5

Chapter 7

How Shall You Escape?

We cannot escape hell, fire, and damnation without the love of Christ. I believe that God casted Satan and his angels out of heaven when they sinned. Satan tried to be equal with God and convinced one third of the angels to follow him (Revelation 12:9). If God would cast angels out of heaven because of an evil thought, we certainly have no chance of getting into heaven in our sinful state. I hate to sound harsh, but this is the word of God and if I am going to help you, I can't cut any corners, I have to tell you as the scripture says. God is HOLY, RIGHTEOUS, GOOD, TRUE, POWERFUL, and ALMIGHTY. He won't tolerate sin from anyone: not from His angels, not from Adam and Eve, and not from us. Not in heaven, and not on earth. We have to conform to His way, He won't conform to ours.

We serve a righteous God He is fair in all of His ways He hasn't asked us to do anything that we can't do. He is the only righteous God and He has commanded us to love Him, and only Him. To love Him is to keep His commandments. To keep His commandments is to live free from sin. There are no ifs, ands, or buts, about it, it is very clear. We have to obey God to escape hell. *For if God spared not the angels that sinned, but cast them down to hell and delivered them into chains of darkness, to be reserved unto judgment; and spared not the old world, but saved Noah the eighth person, a preacher of righteousness, bringing in the flood upon the world of the ungodly; and turning the cities of Sodom and Gomorrah into ashes condemned them with an overthrow, making them an example unto those that after should live ungodly; and delivered just Lot, vexed with the filthy conversation of the wicked: (For that righteous man dwelling among them, in seeing and hearing, vexed his righteous soul from day to day with their unlawful deeds.) The Lord knoweth how to deliver the godly out of temptations, and to reserve the unjust unto the Day of Judgment to be punished* (II PETER 2:4-9). God created mankind to be holy, without sin, like Him, but since Satan deceived Eve and continues to deceive mankind today, God has made this an individual walk with Him. We each have to repent and surrender to God's will.

We don't have to be deceived by Satan anymore and cast into hell and delivered into the chains of darkness. I Peter 1:15&16, *But as he which hath called you is holy, so be ye holy in all manner of conversation; because it is written, BE YE HOLY; FOR I AM HOLY.* He wouldn't have told us to be holy if He knew we could not do it. God has ALL power in his hand. He can keep you righteous and holy in this present world according to His Word if you want to be kept. Being righteous or holy according to man's way of thinking is doing everything just right or being "holier than thou". That is not God's way. God's way is upholding His commandments, and submitting to the Holy Spirit.

God has made it so simple and has given ample opportunity for us to make the decision to follow Him. You are not your own you were bought with a price – the blood of Jesus. You belong to God, and He loves you. And because He loves you, He sends people to prepare you for your eternal destination. So, despite what you may have been taught or what you may believe, you will not escape hell if you do not change your life before God comes back or before you leave this earth some other way. You have to come out of your sin now before it is too late.

Satan is as real as God and he is trying to take as many souls as he can to hell with him and his angels. Think about it, if God did not spare Satan and a third of the angles once they sinned and put them out of heaven, why should we think He is going to allow us into heaven in our sin? Judgment Day is coming. Don't let it be said too late that your name is not written in the Lamb's Book of Life. You have the opportunity right now to confess Jesus Christ as your Lord and Savior.

Apostle Paul said in Romans 12:1, that it's a reasonable service. *I beseech you therefore, brethren, by the mercies of God, that ye present your bodies a living sacrifice, holy, acceptable unto God, which is your reasonable service.* God asks so little of us, yet He gave so much! It should be enough for anybody to have a change of heart and mind once they have read or heard of the great sacrifice that Jesus made for mankind. Jesus at least deserves your respect enough to try. I beseech you today, don't let His sacrifice be in vain.

Isaiah 53:3-7 describes in more details Jesus' sacrifice: *He is despised and rejected of men; a man of sorrows, and acquainted with grief; and we hid as it were our faces from him; he was despised, and we esteemed him not. Surely, he hath borne our griefs, and carried our sorrows: yet we did esteem him stricken, smitten of God, and afflicted. But he was wounded for our transgressions, he was bruised for our iniquities: the chastisement of our peace was upon him; and with his stripes we are healed. All we like sheep have gone astray, we have turned every one to his own way; and the Lord hath laid on him the iniquity of us all. He was oppressed, and he was afflicted, yet he opened not his mouth: he is*

*brought as a lamb to the slaughter, and as a sheep before her
shearers is dumb, so he openeth not his mouth.* Jesus was
beaten all night. A crown of thorns was pressed down
on His head. He was spat on, slapped, and mocked. His
hairs were pulled from His beard, and He was speared
in the side and He died for you.

I urge you to start calling on Jesus now to thank Him
and establish a relationship with Him before you are
in trouble. Then, when you need Him most, He will be
right there for you. You will have built up a storehouse
of blessings and He will be there when you need Him.
There is power in the name of Jesus. Acts 4:12 says,
*Neither is there salvation in any other; for there is none other
name under heaven given among men, whereby we must be
saved.* So many without hope that either didn't know
how to call on His name or refused to believe in His
name, have committed suicide. Beloved one, you don't
have to ever be in that position. Just believe in Jesus.

As long as you have breath in your body there is hope.
Never give up! God knows all about you and He cares
for you. All of your prayers will be answered according
to the purpose He has for your life. You will never see
a day where your everyday needs are not met. God's
way brings peace, love, joy, happiness into your life.
Contentment and understanding come when you do it
God's way. Beloved one, what I am saying, is that all you
need is in Jesus. It doesn't matter how old or how young
you are God wants to save you.

Most young people think they are invincible, but you
have to know that you did not give yourself life, nor
can you sustain your own life. God's grace and mercy
are the only reasons we all are still living. God has been
extremely merciful and has given us ample time to get
our souls right with Him. This world is in such chaos
and turmoil, I know that God is sick of the wicked ways
of man. When this world comes to an end, will you be

found in His grace, and not pleading for mercy because you are headed to the lake of fire?

God destroyed the world with water in Noah's day (Genesis 6:17 says, *And, Behold, I, even I, do bring a flood of waters upon the earth, to destroy all flesh, wherein is the breath of life, from under heaven; and every thing that is in the earth shall die.* He has said that He will destroy the world again but with fire this time. Matthew 13:41-43 says, *The Son of man shall send forth his angels, and they shall gather out of his kingdom all things that offend, and them which do iniquity; and shall cast them into a furnace of fire: there shall be wailing and gnashing of teeth. Then shall the righteous shine forth as the sun in the kingdom of their Father. Who hath ears to hear, let him hear.* Verses 49-50 says, *So shall it be at the end of the world: the angels shall come forth, and sever the wicked from among the just, and shall cast them into the furnace of fire: there shall be wailing and gnashing of teeth.* God is real. He has the power and He will cast you into a lake of fire if you do not take heed to His word. Oh, but you can be one of the righteous that shine forth as the sun in the kingdom of their Father and be with Him in glory. Please take heed, this may be your last warning.

God is omniscient, omnipresent, and omnipotent: He knows all things, is everywhere at all times, and is all powerful. There is no secret that you can keep from Him. The Father, Son, and the Holy Spirit know all. What is done in the dark will eventually come to the light: it will be shown on the housetop. Beloved one, when you are doing something wrong that you think no one will know about, God knows. He even knows the secrets of your heart. God will shine a light on you and, unfortunately, it will usually hurt you and your loved ones. Read the story of David and Bath-Sheba, II Samuel 11:12 says, *For thou didst it secretly: but I will do this thing before all Israel, and before the sun.* He will also show your wrongdoings before the sun for all to see. The temporary pleasure is not worth the price that you will have to pay. Living in the moment not preparing for your future is careless. What you think is living and enjoying life now will cost you an eternal life of pain later.

God deserves our love, respect, and obedience, he took pride in creating us. David said in Psalmss 139:14, *I will praise thee; for I am fearfully and wonderfully made: marvelous are thy works; and that my soul knoweth right well.* There is no escaping God's presence. He created you and knows all about you. Psalmss 139:1-13, *O Lord, thou hast searched me, and know me. Thou knowest my downsitting and mine uprising; thou understandest my thought afar off. Thou compassest my path and my lying down, and art acquainted with all my ways. For there is not a word in my tongue, but, lo, O Lord, thou knowest it altogether. Thou hast beset me behind and before and laid thine hand upon me. Such knowledge is too wonderful for me; it is high, I cannot attain unto it. Whither shall I go from thy spirit? Or whither shall I flee from thy presence? If I ascend up into heaven, thou art there: if I make my bed in hell, behold, thou art there. If I take the wings of the morning, and dwell in the uttermost parts of the sea; Even there shall thy hand lead me, and thy right hand shall hold me. If I say, Surely the darkness shall cover me; even the night shall be light about me. Yea, the darkness hideth not from thee; but the night shineth as the day: the darkness and the light are both alike to thee. For thou hast possessed my reins: thou hast covered me in my mother's womb.* So, you see there is no place that you can hide from God so make your ways and thoughts right with him.

Prepare yourself for that promise spoken of in 2 Peter 3:13, . . . *new heavens and a new earth, wherein dwelleth righteousness.* The new heaven is the New Testament, the new and living way, wherein lies life; and the new earth is you becoming a new creature dwelling in righteousness.God formed us from the earth and our bodies will return to the earth.We are earthly creatures that have to become new spiritual creatures in Christ Jesus.

For to be carnally minded is death; but to be spiritually minded is life and peace. Because the carnal mind is enmity against God: for it is not subject to the law of God, neither indeed can be. So then they that are in the flesh cannot please God. But ye are not in the flesh, but in the Spirit, if so be that the Spirit of God dwell in you. Now if any man have not the Spirit of Christ, he is none of his. And if Christ be in you, the body is dead because of sin; but the Spirit is life because of righteousness. But if the Spirit of him that raised up Jesus from the dead dwell in you, he that raised up Christ from the dead shall also quicken your mortal bodies by his Spirit that dwelleth in you. Therefore, brethren, we are debtors, not to the flesh, to live after the flesh. For if ye live after the flesh, ye shall die: but if ye through the Spirit do mortify the deeds of the body, ye shall live. For as many as are led by the Spirit of God, they are the sons of God. **Romans 8:6-14**

Chapter 8

Love Yourself

I will praise thee; for I am fearfully and wonderfully made; marvelous are thy works; and that my soul knoweth right well. **Psalms 139:14**

God loves you or He wouldn't have given you this awesome opportunity to get back to Him through his Son, Jesus. Love yourself enough to save your very life from hell, fire and damnation. You can do it – the Word says we can save ourselves from this untoward generation (Acts 2:40). Love yourself enough to give yourself permission to allow God to save your soul. No one else can do it for you. Only you can choose it.

The Apostle Paul in 2 Corinthians 12:8-10 had a situation that was a thorn in his flesh. Paul besought the Lord to remove whatever it was that was a constant source of distraction for him. He prayed and asked God three times to allow it to depart from him, but God did not take it away. God wanted Paul to trust Him and to know that His grace was sufficient for him and through His power and strength He would provide whatever Paul's need was. In this particular passage, I also believe that God allowed that thorn to remain in Paul's flesh so that Paul wouldn't allow his position and the great revelation of the word that he had received from the Lord to lift him up higher than what he needed to be as a man.

God is a present help in our time of need as He was in Paul's time of need. After the third petition to God Paul understood that God would see him through whatever situation he was in the same as He will see us through our trials and tribulations if we trust in Him. God is able to keep us saved, holy, and set apart from the sins of the world. We still have to go through trials and tribulations because we are human and this is a curse of sin, but we can go through them with joy in our hearts and praises on our lips knowing that God will deliver us. The key is to truly know and believe that God can do it.

By the Holy Spirit, we have the power to defeat every enemy. Love yourself enough to petition God to receive His Spirit, to strengthen you, and to give you understanding. It's vital that you pray and establish a relationship with God. God is our source of power and strength. I love this scripture, Paul said, . . .*Most gladly therefore will I rather glory in my infirmities, that the power of Christ may rest upon me. Therefore I take pleasure in infirmities, in reproaches, in necessities, in persecutions, in distresses for Christ's sake: for when I am weak, then am I strong* (2 Corinthians 12:9-10). I had to come to this point in my life during a long, ten-year period of struggling financially. I hadn't remembered this scripture, but one day I read it again, and it blessed my soul. This is exactly how I felt and confessed it to the Lord. Paul suffered something in the flesh as we must do, and I did.

I was the one in the family that always had money and was able to help everyone. So, when I became financially destitute it was a very hard pill for me to swallow. God knows all about us and he knows just what it takes to bring us to our knees in prayer. He more than brought me to my knees – and I thank him for it! I wouldn't be where I am right now in my spirit and soul if it had not been for that trial. This may not make sense, but there is beauty in our suffering. Our suffering causes us to have to call on God for help, thus, bringing us closer to God. It is God/Jesus that is available to see us through. It's unfortunate that we have to find that out the hard way, but, when you know that there is nothing too hard for God – you can live a saved life in this present world. I implore you, give yourself the gift of life, love yourself, you are worth it!

I want you to understand that you don't have to suffer unnecessarily. All the struggles and hardships that you are experiencing don't have to be. God will bless you day by day to have all that you need in life. God will provide the peace and joy that you seek. He will give you the desires of your heart if you will love yourself enough to give yourself to Him. Allow God to come into your heart, your mind, your soul. It is just that easy beloved one, ask God to come into your life and fill you with His Spirit. He loves you!

Once you start to love yourself, you can love others right with the love of God. You will treat other people the way you want to be treated. Constant stressing or anxiety will lessen. Beloved one, all of your life struggles are determined by the way you live and perceive life. Most times we have difficulty with others because we haven't figured out how to love ourselves. We feel life is hard because we won't allow God to come in and help us. I've been there, so I can tell you that there is a better way and all you have to do is love yourself enough to find that better life.

Most of us have family who love us but nobody in this life can love you like you can love yourself. Your life should be the most precious and important thing to you. It is to God. God said you are wonderfully made.

Believe that and stand in your right to be a beautiful creature in God. If you walk in your truth with the Lord on your side how powerful would you be? Loving the Lord is freeing, beloved one, you haven't had a peaceful mind or have felt so good in your spirit until you experience the power of the Holy Spirit. By loving yourself and loving God/Jesus, there are endless possibilities in this life.

Ye that love the LORD, hate evil: he preserveth the souls of his saints; he delivereth them out of the hand of the wicked.
Psalms 97:10

Chapter 9

Talk to God

Every human being in their right mind has thought or wondered about God, or how it is that we came to be. I am a simple human being, a nobody to most people, but even I have questioned where I came from and how this world came to be. I know without having to read the Bible that there has to be a God. There has to be someone or something greater or higher than us. We, this world, didn't just appear. Where there is a creature there must be a creator. Both the creature and the creator had or needed some kind of a relationship. We all have a connection with our God we have to recognize it and nurtured it before it can develop into a true relationship.

We must take the time to meditate on God and be inquisitive about life and our purpose here. That is our beginning to a relationship with God. You have to go to him in prayer and the Bible for the answers you seek. No one person has all the answers. The only one who can answer your questions satisfactorily is God. God can and He will satisfy your curiosity. When you can't talk to your family and friends, you can talk to God. Morning, noon, or night, He is there waiting to develop that relationship with you. You don't have to wait until you can be alone, or until you go to church. You don't have to wait until you change your life, just start talking to Him. You don't have to talk out loud or with big enticing words. You don't have to weep and mourn, just talk to Him. You can talk to Him in your mind, or in your bed, or on bending knees. It doesn't matter how you do it, He just wants you to talk to Him. As communication is vital in any relationship, it is also vital between you and God. Communicate with God/Jesus through prayer, song, praise, any time that you can give thought to your Creator is of uttermost importance. Take your burdens to the Lord in prayer. Communicate with God when you are happy or have questions.

Most times we seek answers to our problems from the wrong people. We seek people we trust and whose opinion we value. We take what they say as law. They may mean well, but their answers could steer us in the wrong direction because they can't comprehend God's plan and purpose for our life.

The human bond between a parent and a child is great. From working with foster children, I have learned that no matter how bad of a life a child has with their biological parent, they would rather remain in that life as long as they can be with their parents. The desire to be with a biological parent is something unique from God. He instilled the bond in us so that we would have a greater love for our parents, creating a family unit. God desires for us to have an even greater connection with Him. We won't be satisfied in this life until we do. All of our emotions came from God so we have to go to God to connect with him in order to fill our souls with what we need. Your inner man needs to connect with its source of life. You need Jesus beloved one, He is the way, the truth, and the life.

You will not know what it is to be truly happy and

to have real joy until you find Jesus. Sure, you do this and that, you go here and there. You inhale or digest this and that, you have him or her, you may even have a brand-new car or a pocket full of money. All of that is temporary happiness. *"...For the joy of the Lord is your strength"* (Nehemiah 8:10). When you get joy from the Lord it stays with you even in your hardest times because the joy is in your soul. You won't need any of those crutches to try and fulfill your needs. God will fill you with inner peace and satisfaction. As you become disciplined and content, you will be filled with the Holy Spirit of God. Once you submit to God, the world can offer you a million dollars to turn back, but you will say," No thank you, give me Jesus!"

It's not too late, make your choice now. *And if it seem evil unto you to serve the Lord, choose you this day whom ye will serve; whether the gods which our fathers served that were on the other side of the flood, or the gods of the Amorites, in whose land ye dwell* . . . (Joshua 24:15). This applies to us as well we can't have it both ways. Either we live unto God or we live unto Satan. You have to choose you can't serve them both at the same time. God can't tolerate sin. You have to make the choice, God won't do it for you. Choose life, beloved one. I promise you, it will be the best decision that you will ever make.

Once you make up your mind, just take one day at a time. The past is gone, tomorrow is not promised. Today is here, right now. In your present state of mind, just believe. Remain in constant communication with the Lord – praying, singing, reading. Prayer is essential, it will give you strength each day to continue your walk with the Lord. When you are feeling weak or wondering if this is the right path that you should take, talk directly to God. He will guide you and comfort your heart. Once you pray and talk with Jesus the weight will be lifted, and the more you communicate with Him the joy and peace will come. Before you know it, you will have joy unspeakable!

Now, I must warn you, that if you do not establish a relationship with God, there will be consequences. You will incur the wrath of God. I can't just tell you of all the good and not warn you of the consequences. It would defeat my purpose of reaching out to you and wouldn't help you in making a sound decision about your soul. "How shall we escape?" We cannot escape, there is no place that we can hide from the Lord. Saved or unsaved we will answer to God one day. *Marvel not at this: for the hour is coming, in the which all that are in the graves shall hear his voice, And shall come forth; they that have done good, unto the resurrection of life; and they that have done evil, unto the resurrection of damnation* (St. John 5:29-30). Hear his voice now talk to him now while you are in your right mind, strong, and healthy so that He can use you to advance the Kingdom. Once you are in the grave it is too late. When you hear His voice from the grave it will be to sentence you to either everlasting damnation or to the resurrection of life. Eternal life in Jesus, imagine how beautiful, serene it will be.

When He calls your name don't you want Him to say, *Well done, thou good and faithful servant* . . . (Matthew 25:21), and don't you want to be written in the Lamb's book of life? *But they which are written in the Lamb's book of life* (Revelation 21:27). That will only happen if you surrender your all to Him. Bow your head, bend your knee: confess your love to the Lord and let Him know that you are sorry for your sins and are now ready to turn your life over to him. It's as easy as saying, "Here I am Lord, I surrender my all to you. I love you Jesus and I want to live for you." The angels will rejoice in Heaven.

God/Jesus is alive you can talk to Him as you would anyone else that you would pour your heart out to. St. John 5:26-27 says, *For as the Father hath life in himself; so hath he given to the Son to have life in himself; And hath given him authority to execute judgment also, because he is the Son of man.* I find it easy to communicate with the Lord in thought/mind, but I also go on my knees and verbally talk to Him. There is no wrong way to communicate with God as long as you do it with honor. I love talking to Jesus, and I long for the day that He executes judgment upon me, I know the life that I live before Him and as long as I am in my right mind, I am going to strive to make it to heaven.

Please believe that God is alive and will communicate with you through His Holy Spirit. Though the Lord doesn't communicate with us the way He did with Moses and the children of Israel verbally, He has allowed the Holy Spirit to move on His behalf. *And ye said, Behold, the Lord our God hath showed us his glory and his greatness, and we have heard his voice out of the midst of the fire: we have seen this day that God doth talk with man, and he liveth* (Deuteronomy 5:24). You have to believe that God is God and He can do anything. He will hear you. All that you have to do is be sincere in your communication with Him. As he led and saved the children of Israel, He will do the same for you.

And the Lord heard the voice of your words, when ye spake unto me; and the Lord said unto me, I have heard the voice of the words of this people, which they have spoken unto thee: they have well said all that they have spoken. O that there were such a heart in them, that they would fear me, and keep all my commandments always, that it might be well with them, and with their children for ever. **Deuteronomy 5:28-29**

Chapter 10

Prayer

I pray that I have persuaded you to seek the Lord. I pray that I have said something that has stirred your mind and heart to the point that you want to say, "What must I do to be saved?" I pray that you will at least consider that Jesus is Lord and King, Savior of your soul!

Will you please pray this beautiful prayer with me and mean it from within your heart?

A Prayer for Cleansing

Have mercy upon me, O God, according to thy loving kindness: according unto the multitude of thy tender mercies blot out my transgressions. Wash me thoroughly from mine iniquity, and cleanse me from my sin. For I acknowledge my transgressions: and my sin is ever before me. Against thee, thee only, have I sinned, and done this evil in thy sight: that thou mightiest be justified when thou speakest, and be clear when thou judgest. Behold, I was shapen in iniquity; and in sin did my mother conceive me. Behold, thou desirest truth in the inward parts: and in the hidden part thou shalt make me to know wisdom. Purge me with hyssop, and I shall be clean: wash me, and I shall be whiter than snow. Make me to hear joy and gladness; that the bones which thou has broken may rejoice. Hide thy face from my sins, and blot out all mine iniquities. Create in me a clean heart, O God; and renew a right spirit within me . . . **Psalms 51:1-10**

Learn the Lord's Prayer, Jesus instructed. The Lord's prayer covers every aspect in life.

The LORD'S Prayer

Our Father which art in heaven, hallowed be thy name. Thy kingdom come. Thy will be done in earth, as it is in heaven. Give us this day our daily bread. And forgive us our debts, as we forgive our debtors. And lead us not into temptation, but deliver us from evil: for thine is the kingdom, and the power, and the glory, forever, Amen. **Matthew 6:9-13**

Chapter 11

May God Ever Bless You

Whatever you have gone through in your life that has caused you to feel about yourself the way that you do, pray to God, put it in His hands. Let it go so that you can live the rest of your life free as the person that God intended you to be before that thing happened to you. Your problems and situations in life happened to make you a stronger better person. Take what you have been given in life thus far and become a better you, then help somebody else.

Beloved one, I have given you what was in my heart because I love you and truly want to see you happy and saved. We are living in such a time that I feel it necessary to pour out my heart. As Scripture has said, *Except the Lord of hosts had left unto us a very small remnant,* . . . (Isaiah 1:9). You can be among that saved remnant and live eternally with Jesus. I pray that God will ever bless you and keep you in his care. When you get time, read the book of Psalmss. It is so beautiful. The songs of David will ease your burdens, lift your spirits, and put joy in your heart. God bless you!!!

I have preached righteousness in the great congregation: Lo, I have not refrained by lips, O Lord, thou knowest. I have not hid thy righteousness within my heart; I have declared thy faithfulness and thy salvation: I have not concealed thy loving kindness and thy truth from the great congregation. **Psalms 40:9-10**

I love you. I want you to be saved and live a happy life now and for eternity. God loves you and wants to receive you into His kingdom for an eternity of Love!

Scriptures

I would like to leave you a few scriptures to research that will give you confidence and support.

Acts 4:12 *Neither is there salvation in any other: for there is none other name under heaven given among men, whereby we must be saved.*

Deuteronomy 17:18 – 20 *And it shall be, when he sitteth upon the throne of his kingdom, that he shall write him a copy of this law in a book out of that which is before the priests the Levites: And it shall be with him, and he shall read therein all the days of his life: that he may learn to fear the Lord his God, to keep all the words of this law and these statutes, to do them: That his heart be not lifted up above his brethren, and that he turn not aside from the commandment, to the right hand, or to the left: to the end that he may prolong his days in his kingdom, he, and his children, and in the midst of Israel.*

Hebrews 13:17 *Obey them that have the rule over you, and submit yourselves: for they watch for your souls, as they that must give account, that they may do it with joy, and not with grief: for that is unprofitable for you.*

Matthew 19:25-26 *When his disciples heard it, they were exceedingly amazed, saying, who then can be saved? But Jesus beheld them, and said unto them, with men this is impossible; but with God all things are possible.*

John 10:9-11 *I am the door: by me if any man enter in, he shall be saved, and shall go in and out, and find pasture. The thief cometh not, but for to steal, and to kill, and to destroy: I am come that they might have life, and that they might have it more abundantly. I am the good shepherd: the good shepherd giveth his life for the sheep.*

Jude 1:24-25 *Now unto him that is able to keep you from falling, and to present you faultless before the presence of his glory with exceeding joy, To the only wise God our Savior, be glory and majesty dominion and power, both now and ever. Amen.*

I Peter 4:1-2 *FORASMUCH then as Christ hath suffered for us in the flesh, arm yourselves likewise with the same mind: for he that hath suffered in the flesh hath ceased from sin; that he no longer should live the rest of his time in the flesh to the lusts of men, but to the will of God.*

I John 2:15-16 *Love not the world, neither the things that are in the world. If any man love the world, the love of the Father is not in him. For all that is in the world, the lust of the flesh, and the lust of the eyes, and the pride of life, is not of the Father, but is of the world. And the world passeth away, and the lust thereof: but he that doeth the will of God abideth for ever.*

St. John 15: 5-7 *I am the vine, ye are the branches: He that abideth in me, and I in him, the same bringeth forth much fruit: for without me ye can do nothing. If a man abide not in me, he is cast forth as a branch, and is withered; and men gather them, and cast them into the fire, and they are burned. If ye abide in me, and my words abide in you, ye shall ask what ye will, and it shall be done unto you.*

II Corinthians 7:1 *Having therefore these promises, dearly beloved, let us cleanse ourselves from all filthiness of the flesh and spirit, perfecting holiness in the fear of God.*

Romans 12:1- 2 *I BESEECH you therefore, brethren, by the mercies of God, that ye present your bodies a living sacrifice, holy acceptable unto God, which is your reasonable service. And be not conformed to this world: but be ye transformed by the renewing of your mind, that ye may prove what is that good, and acceptable, and perfect, will of God.*

Joshua 24:15 *An if it seem evil unto you to serve the Lord, choose you this day whom ye will serve; whether the gods which your fathers served that were on the other side of the flood, or the gods of the Amorites, in whose land ye dwell: but as for me and my house, we will serve the Lord.*

Jude 1:5-7 *I will therefore put you in remembrance, through ye once knew this, how that the Lord, having saved the people out of the land of Egypt, afterward destroyed them that believed not. And the angels which kept not their first estate, but left their own habitation, he hath reserved in everlasting chains under darkness unto the judgment of the great day. Even as Sodom and Gomorrah, and the cities about them in like manner, giving themselves over to fornication, and going after strange flesh, are set forth for an example, suffering the vengeance of eternal fire.*

Proverbs 30:11-14 *There is a generation that curseth their father, and doth not bless their mother. There is a generation that are pure in their own eyes, and yet is not washed from their filthiness. There is a generation, O how lofty are their eyes! And their eyelids are lifted up. There is a generation whose teeth are as swords, and their jaw teeth as knives, to devour the poor from off the earth, and the needy from among men.*

Romans 6:23 *For the wages of sin is death; but the gift of God is eternal life through Jesus Christ our Lord.*

2 Peter 3:13 *Nevertheless we, according to his promise, look for new heavens and a new earth, wherein dewelleth righteousness.*

Luke 18:29-30 *And he said unto them, verily I say unto you, there is no man that hath left house, or parents, or brethren, or wife, or children, for the Kingdom of God's sake, who shall not receive manifold more in this present time, and in the world to come life everlasting.*

Colossians 3:5-6 *Mortify therefore your members which are upon the earth; fornication, uncleanness, inordinate affection, evil concupiscence, and covetousness, which is idolatry: For which things' sake the wrath of God cometh on the children of disobedience . . .*

I LOVE YOU
BUT GOD LOVES US MORE

God loves us more
He created us in His likeness and image
Of course, He's going to adore
He so loved the world
He gave His only begotten Son
Because He loves us more
And now you worship Him through Spirit
Until your work here on earth is done
He loves us so unconditionally
It pierces right through the core
But if a person falls by the way
He'll put your blessings in store
Without the relationship with God
Your life will be a bore
You should always kneel and praise Him
Until the bend of your knees are sore
All we have to do is knock
And He'll open up the door
His Spirit can fill a room
From the ceiling to the floor
We're judged according to how we live our life
And this is something we should never ignore
On that great day of judgement
He's taking us back to where we were before
His creation should always love each other
But remember God loves us more

BRANDON DWAYNE MARABLE, SR.

About the Author

NINA P. PRINGLE was born in Erin, Tennessee in 1960 and moved to Oakland, California at the age of 8-years-old. Being the fifth of twelve children, she was raised with great family values that enabled her to be a good mother and wife. She was married in 1982 to a wonderful man, and have 3 beautiful children and 7 grandchildren. She has served the Lord for 37-years and is now looking for the Lord to bless her writing ministry.

Nina can be reached via e-mail:
Nppringle@comcast.net
HOLYCDR@COMCAST.NET

"ALL THINGS ARE POSSIBLE TO HIM THAT BELIEVETH"
Mark 9:23

www.ingramcontent.com/pod-product-compliance
Lightning Source LLC
Chambersburg PA
CBHW031555040426
42452CB00006B/312